A STONE IN MY SHOE

A Stone in My Shoe

IN SEARCH OF NEIGHBOURHOOD

George Ellenbogen

Véhicule Press

Published with the generous assistance of The Canada Council for the
Arts and the Canada Book Fund of the Department of Canadian Heritage.

Cover design: David Drummond
Set in Adobe Minion by Simon Garamond
Printed by Marquis Book Printing Inc.

LIBRARY AND ARCHIVES CANADA CATALOGUING IN PUBLICATION

Ellenbogen, George, 1934-, author
A stone in my shoe : in search of neighbourhood /
George Ellenbogen.

ISBN 978-1-55065-356-4 (pbk.)

1. Ellenbogen, George, 1934-. 2. Poets, Canadian (English)–Québec
(Province)–Montréal–Biography. 3. Montréal (Québec)–Biography.
I. Title.

PS8559.L542Z65 2013   C811.54   C2013-905907-5

Published by Véhicule Press, Montréal, Québec, Canada
www.vehiculepress.com

Distribution in Canada by LitDistCo
www.litdistco.ca

Distribution in the U.S. by Independent Publishers Group
www.ipgbook.com

Printed in Canada on FSC certified paper.

Contents

Acknowledgements

I NEVER MET GRANDFATHER David, who died of typhus during World War II, nor was I aware at the time that I had a Romanian grandfather. His wife, Pessie, who carried herself majestically, I met only briefly in New York on her way to Peru after she had been spirited out of the USSR. They did not surface in my life like my mother's sister, Aunt Faige, and their mother, Baba Rose, but they are now among those who fill in the picture that hangs prominently in my memory. I can enter their lives as a familiar, sit around their tables, eavesdrop on their conversations.

A multitude of family members, friends, and perfect strangers have helped to create that picture which appears on the following pages. With so many to thank, it is possible that a slip of memory will cause me to overlook a contributor who deserves my gratitude. My apologies in advance. For those who felt that their contributions were minor, let me say that every recovered detail helped me move forward. Many were provided by members of my family: Esther Marco, Ben Berman, Klara Landman, Gustavo Gorriti, Edith Gorriti Tsouri, Becky Lender, Ruth Lender, Sylvia Dolitsky, Carl Laxer, and my brother, Irving Ellenbogen.

A number of books on Montreal's Jewish community helped to explain my parents' initial impressions of Montreal. Israel Medres's *Montreal of Yesterday* and *Between the Wars* treat so many aspects of the Jewish community that I came to see them as course texts in Montreal's Jewish history. Also helpful were Joseph Graham's conversations and his richly detailed *Naming the Laurentians*; also *Through the Eyes of the Eagle, An Every Day Miracle, Storied Streets, Baron Byng to Bagels, Renewing our Days, City Unique, A Street Called the Main,* an article on political and social slants in secondary school education by Tamara Myers and Mary-Anne Poutanen, and the thesis that earned Judith Seidel an MA at McGill in 1932.

Simon Dardick and Nancy Marrelli, the publishers of several of the books above, were generous in so many ways, especially in providing useful leads.

A breakfast conversation with Stanley Asher introduced me to basic research vehicles; without them, I would have been limited to my photo albums and memories. Janice Rosen of the Canadian Jewish Congress Archives and Shannon Hodge of the Jewish Public Library Archives often steered me to materials that, I later realized, were indispensable. And the observations Pierre Anctil provided in conversations and email exchanges became a map that I followed with utter faith. He is indisputably the expert on Jewish Montreal, and the community is blessed by his willingness to share his insights. Professor Nicholas Evans of the University of Hull (UK) put his expertise on immigration at my disposal; thus I was able to track my mother's journey from Gora Kalwaria to Canada.

The intimacy of community that I felt over sixty years ago returned when I interviewed residents of my old neighborhood: Frances Karanofsky, Eunice Seligson and her sister Malke, and Jack Labow; my Baron Byng schoolmates, Harvey Yarosky QC and the Hon. Joseph Nuss, who also shared memories of the Buzz Beurling Memorial Club and a number of photos including one of the 1945 Montreal Canadians' championship hockey team. For some splendid photos of Boulevard St. Laurent, I am indebted to André Vigneau of the Société de Transport de Montréal.

I am grateful to fiction writers, Juan Alonso and Pierce Butler, for frequent conversations on where the border lay between memoir and fiction; to my daughter, Sara Rachel, for some valuable last minute suggestions; to Yayoi Miya Rosenkranz and Richard Kyte who solved my frequent computer problems and to the Virginia Center for the Creative Arts for several residencies which enabled me to devote my full attention to this project.

Even with all this support, I could not have written this book without the guidance of three remarkable women. Dr. Mary Seeman, one of Canada's distinguished scientists as well as a classmate at McGill, taught me how to work with genealogical records, and whenever my efforts subsided, she provided me with new approaches. Montreal's eminent architectural historian, Susan Bronson, walked through my old neighborhood with me and allowed me to witness as she read buildings as easily as one reads a morning newspaper. Virtually every architectural reference in this book traces to her observations. I will not be able to touch this manuscript without remembering the contribution of these two women.

But my greatest debt is to my late partner, the writer, Evelyn Shakir, who read and reread—several times. There is scarcely a page in this book that does not bear her imprint, her suggestions for highlighting what was central and her sculpting to achieve that end, prodding when necessary and encouraging when I became discouraged. She was in at the beginning, urging me to write about my old neighborhood, and, years earlier, reminding me to tape interviews of my parents; and, with her final nod of approval, she was in at the end. It is to her memory that I dedicate this book.

Preface

A Stone in My Shoe: In Search of Neighborhood did not present itself voluntarily; it had to be coaxed. My partner, the late Evelyn Shakir, had urged me to write about the neighborhood that I so frequently described to her. She may have concluded that plunging me head downward into such a project would spare her—or at least reduce—the number of anecdotes that I would flourish on our drives between our Boston home and the Montreal homes of my childhood and adolescence. And so, in preparation, I leafed through old street maps, ship manifests, photo albums, and yellowing newspapers, touching their surfaces to raise a world long gone. As I studied them--passenger lists, photos, and Lovell's Montreal Directory with records dating back to the 1840s—each stretched into its own history and narrative. A house once lived in conjured up adjoining buildings until they became not merely separate structures, but a family of brick, stone and wood with different identities—pharmacy, corner store, button shop, deli, three-flat house—all assembled for a reunion. Similarly, as soon as I recognized family members in the Lovell directory, they refused to remain confined; before I closed the guide, I realized that I had released a slew of relatives into three-dimensionhood; they would return me to where my father shoveled coal in the bowels of a freighter, where my mother sang on the stage of the Monument National, where the Spaniard, Mr. Mora, stared out his exile at Lac Nantel, where neighborhood children slapped a hockey puck until twilight.

I was finally writing the memoir Evelyn had urged upon me, giving her the Montreal of an earlier time. What I didn't realize was that I was giving her something I hadn't planned to, something additional. Although my old Montreal neighborhood meant much to me as I grew into adulthood, and means much to me now, I was celebrating more than nostalgia. The separate montages that emerged and the images they engendered, whether a picture of Jewish children singing "Silent Night," brothers picking berries in the Laurentians, children riveted to the exploits of Rocket Richard on the radio, became portals that opened to one larger montage, in which there was an unceasing call for belonging, neighborhood, community, even when that community was limited to no more than two…or one with an imagination who finds community in forest, mountain, lake, the unassailable brick fronts of row houses, or within one's self.

Without being aware of it, we follow the wisdom of community, a wisdom that emerges from traditional comedy with its suspicion of extremes, recklessness, adventure; its embrace of conviviality, empathy, reconciliation. In response to the daily battering we endure from television and print coverage of war, pestilence, and famine, when visions of perfection recede further and further away, we turn to those rituals, Christmas dinner or Passover Seder, beach outing or block party, that link us to one another, that comfort and reassure. They may not be as titillating as adventure, but like Yeats' wild old wicked man we choose them, "the second best," and survive.

Writers do not always write the book they intend to. What I planned when I rummaged through early memories was a book about my Montreal past, a collection of old neighborhood anecdotes and descriptions. What I ended with was a discovery of neighborhood rituals that sustained me, that sustain millions. Evelyn was probably as surprised as I was at the emergence of this focus. But she certainly recognized it: it had, after all, been the focus of her own work on the Arab American community. Unbeknown to us, we had witnessed our work, though written under the same roof, follow different channels, one Arab American, the other Montreal Jewish; but when they emerged, after flowing through their own subterranean passages, they revealed the same preoccupations, concerns, and aspirations, and, like us, had come to their own special relationship, the relationship that unites disparate neighborhoods and individuals, that of trust and acceptance.

PART ONE

First Light

I AM MOVING FAST backward through photo albums, letters opened sixty years ago, stumbling towards the Montreal I once glided through with imaginary skates, mounting at age five the steep wooden stairs of Mount Royal Elementary School—only the name had a touch of nobility—eventually crossing the frontier of Rachel Street to Baron Byng High. Carried by wind through the ice-walled air, the bearded face of my grandfather descends in a portrait, thundering in silence; parents and aunts and uncles and cousins follow, behind them the turbulence of town and shtetl, sometimes in carts rattling over wheel ruts in cobblestone, sometimes like gulls carried noiselessly on currents of air or, like one mass of flotsam and jetsam, steaming across the Atlantic; bobbing in their wake, matzoh balls and the mysterious sounds of the Torah intoned by young boys around long tables with slender fingers and hair finer than mica. They all surface like dolphins scrambling over boulders across the sandbar of a new continent, some dropping from steerage into strange harbors, swimming like my uncles Meyer and Rudolph to shore. Once there, the bewildered shake the journey from their clothes, the coal dust from the engine room, the cramp from steerage, or, for the more affluent, cake crumbs from the main dining room, and look around, studying the movement of the natives—the Francophones, Anglos, Latinos of the Americas—while following the wisdom of their own hands, sewing cloth, shoveling coal, hammering tin.

Overhead, the stars turn like a merry-go-round as a tidal wave of Jews spreads across Montreal's Plateau neighborhood, a crop extending like acres and acres of wheat or soy beans or corn, without variation it seems. Until we discover that the new arrivals aren't all the same. Some have beards, broad brimmed hats, and chant prayers with a fervor intended to draw heaven to earth; and others, earlier arrivals, are Christian, who, though not part of our play, announce themselves in neon lights among the Jewish shops on

St. Lawrence Boulevard: Sinclair's which fronts Katz's Button Shop and Panyemoshku's grocery as though a truce has been declared. These were the syllables in our atlas, the sights that passed us as we passed our hands over the sandpaper roughness of the lumber yard's concrete wall, the glass front of Schwartz's delicatessen. Within our borders, we shuffled up and down stairs, scuffed corridors for eleven years under the arched eyes of teachers who from a distance were one mass of authority, but close up broke down into categories of shape, size, and ideology. We now recognized incompetents and the thumping disciples of British order, purveyors of imperial scents; but also the occasional teachers who made words and numbers dance, thereby opening the gates to the history, literature, and geography texts that ushered us out of the ghetto. By the time we entered high school, we were no longer intimidated by the raw authority of our masters, though somewhat cowed by the aura of Baron Byng High itself, whose storied history presented itself to us in the plaques and trophies arranged on either side of the principal's office. We grew into the school the way one grows into a suit of clothes passed on by an older brother, familiar, comfortable. Less comfortable was the rabbinical training that waited for us as the sun darkened at the end of each school day. The shtetls our parents had left thousands of miles to the east reemerged as we approached the age of thirteen and trudged towards manhood by climbing the stairs to the second story of a flat two blocks down Clark Street, next to a synagogue. Across the threshold, monitored by the squint of the rabbi's wife, we turned into a room dominated by a long table and a dozen or so adolescent heads with skull caps. The scene smacked of the illicit, like the basement of a church school on Santorini where the clergy practiced sedition for years by teaching Greek under the eyes of the occupying Turks.

Between chants in the synagogue and anglophilic hymns to the Empire, we scavenged for icons wherever we could find them, hoping for a Jew, but settling for what was available. The local arenas gave us Jackie Robinson and Maurice Richard, and if we turned the knob of our Philco radio, voices that ranged from Jack Benny in Beverly Hills to Hop Harrigan in a Nazi concentration camp, all far away from Clark Street where we lived, the parallel street, St. Lawrence, where we shopped, and the connecting streets of Rachel and Duluth. We went to school; our parents went to work. Released from classes, we streamed onto the street and played hockey, football with a stuffed sock, and hide and seek while the girls skipped rope and sang," The wind, the wind, the wind blows high, blowing Raizl to the sky," and our shouts and laughter rose like the mysteries of a Chagall painting into a ghettoless heaven. In a few years our play would move to the Rachel Street Pool Room and the Hollywood Theatre, which offered two features, a cartoon, a travelogue, and the Movietone news. Our passage to adulthood came with vaudeville at the Gayety where we tolerated jugglers and comics for the sake of Lili St. Cyr and Peaches.

Family was our ghetto within a ghetto, a string of relatives beginning with my grandmother, stretching to not quite five feet, but tall enough to accumulate three husbands, bury them, and run the world; and, following close behind, like penguins in a storm, keeping up lest they lose their bearings, aunts and uncles, and more cousins than I could count or name. Most lived within a radius of four city blocks, not so difficult to walk, even in the snow and ice of a Montreal winter, especially when the end of the trek meant a mug of hot cocoa and thickly buttered bread from my uncle's bakery. At Passover, relatives congregated around a long table and assaulted mounds of food, the women's badges of achievement. Here we all found the certitude that comes from a pecking order, one that had more to do with age than education. It would never have occurred to me or to my cousins, clutching our high school diplomas, to contradict our grandmother, whose position as head of the family we accepted as though it had been divinely conferred.

After the 1939-45 war, that certitude was tested and often shredded by the verbal scuffling that took place, whether in high school history classes, Nathan's corner store, or Lester's delicatessen.

Political alternatives rose like fortifications only to be besieged and overrun by shouts, shattering argument, or new events. Too much was happening, like fires on dry grassland spurting here and there, more quickly than we could put them out. The imperial vision of our teachers that sailed across the room like Cecil Rhodes down the coast of Africa seeded our iconoclasm, our resentment of the Empire. And the newly created state of Israel was something we viewed with curiosity and wonder, much like discovering a relative in some remote place. All of these remote places became an atlas of three dimensions at Nathan's corner store against the whoosh of cherry soda that he dispensed along with radical newspapers.

But during the months of summer, it all vanished—the political chatter, Hebrew lessons, street play—as though erased from a blackboard as the family moved into a setting of days as endless as fields, interrupted only by the dotting of a few cows here, a barn there, with only a river as a boundary to suggest that this too would come to an end. The place names changed from year to year—St. Sophie, Lesage, Prefontaine, Val Morin, Nantel—and so did the landscape, but it didn't matter. All that mattered was that we rose by the sun instead of the clock and responded to the energy in our bodies rather than the school's recess bells.

Inevitably, we left high school and our ghetto, a handful of blocks in each direction, never fully understanding the social laws that signaled the time for our departure. But like it or not, we were hatched, ready to integrate into that other world. Each of us needed something to draw us out, to take those first tentative steps from the radiant heat of familiar paths to the professions. For some it was engineering, watching numbers cascade into the girders of buildings, for others it was teasing the law into conceptions of fair play, for several it was science, hovering over a microscope, discovering miniature worlds; for me it was the mysteries of language that, unbeknown to me, had begun to attach themselves to the chatter around the family's festive meals, to the strange shapes of Hebrew characters, to the spiral-staired houses on my path to school until the music slowed and the dance stopped and the lights went out and it all ended and I left that ghetto for McGill University only half a mile west, but further than I could imagine.

Where They Came From,
What They Came With

MY FATHER'S FAMILY has a history of scattering. Even their villages, Yurkovitz and Sadagura, give the impression of shifting tectonic plates. My notes place them first as shtetls of Bukovina, part of Franz Joseph's Austro-Hungarian Empire, which was to become Romania after World War I, the Soviet Union after World War II, and now, part of the Ukraine.

My father's grandfather, Beril, of whom I know little, ran a lumber mill in Sadagura, now on the outskirts of Czernowitz the major city in the region; there he took pride in the hardwood floor of his parlor, the planks cut and milled at his own lumber yard, and, equally, in his daily swim in the Prut River, though his paramount achievement was his election as a town alderman.

His son, my grandfather David, who ran a general store in Yurkovitz, slightly north of Czernowitz, is more real to me and still shadows me in several photographs. In one, so wrinkled that it seems as old as he was when it was taken, he appears in the uniform of an Austro-Hungarian officer, a servant of the state. His sword is cradled against his thigh, the tip beside his boot, the hilt under the pocket of his army jacket. He is grim, the corners of his mouth turned down, the portrait of an officer doing his duty, who would prefer to be doing something else; but responsibility does not exclude compassion. One day during the Great War when food was scarce, the shelves almost bare, a horse and wagon pulled up to his general store. It was loaded with vegetables—potatoes, turnips, beets, cabbages—food that could sustain a family for months. When my grandparents asked about the reason for this generosity, those in the wagon reminded them of a kindness that my grandfather had done. When their father, Lieutenant X, was in a position of authority, he had treated my grandfather badly. Eventually grandfather was promoted above him, with ample opportunity to settle old scores. He chose not to. Lieutenant X and his family had not forgotten.

Grandfather David in the uniform of an Austro-Hungarian officer.

Grandfather David and Grandmother Pessie,
Czernowitz.

In a later photo, grandfather David is standing beside my grandmother on a street in Czernowitz. Romanian Gothic figures, their hands at their sides, they look straight ahead, behind them trees shade a park. The photo was taken in the late thirties with war impending, but they seem untroubled, almost smiling, although they are now separated by an ocean from all their children. They have accepted their circumstances.

The last photo I have of him was taken in April 1940, again on a street in Czernowitz, but this time with my uncle Rudolph, who has returned from Lima to urge his father and mother to flee. The impending danger must have been apparent to my grandfather even before Rudolph pressed the point. Although he could not have foreseen droves of Jews herded and crammed into cattle cars, bound for the camp at Transnistria, and forced to walk for several weeks when the Dniester flooded the tracks, the anti-Jewish fervor in Eastern Europe was palpable.

Even before the Nazi invasion and the deportation of Jews under General Ion Antonescu's regime in 1941 and 1942, the fascist Iron Guard had become an intimidating force and restrictions on Jews, for example forbidding their marriage to Christians, had begun. (Later, propaganda minister, Mihai Antonescu would argue at a meeting of the Council of Ministers that in order to purify certain districts Jews would have "to be thrown over the border.")

The case for flight as Rudolph would have set it forth was compelling. But inward voices protested against leaving a circle of friends to settle among strangers who spoke a strange tongue. My grandparents stayed. Meanwhile, war was closing corridors back to Peru. No longer able to exit through the West, Rudolph and his new bride took the Trans-Siberian train from Moscow to Vladivostok. With only some hidden gold coins to sustain them after the Soviets had seized their other valuables, even their wedding bands, they made their way to Yokahama before boarding the *Rokyu Maru* (later sunk) from Japan to Peru. Almost two years after the Nazis entered Romania on October 7, 1940, vehicles cruising the streets of Czernowitz blared demands that

Jews assemble for relocation. Rather than appear as instructed at the railway station on Bahnhofstrasse, the aging couple resigned themselves to a death in their own flat on 3 Marechal Foch, on their own native soil. Arriving a few days later, the postman was puzzled when, still hunkered down, these two Jews responded to his questions with a shrug. He accepted a monthly stipend to keep silent.

My father's life had begun in Yurkovitz in 1905, but after opposing armies swept through his village in the Great War there was little left to salvage, and his family—parents, three older brothers, and three younger sisters—moved to Czernowitz. No longer the owner of a general store, my grandfather barely eked out a living as a broker for produce brought in from farms in the surrounding countryside. His sons did errands to add their pittance to his. When it became apparent that their combined efforts could not support the family, my father and his brothers—Motl, Rudolph, and Meyer—left home; the girls-Dora, Sally, and Ellie remained.

In the first photo I have of my father, taken as he is leaving Czernowitz, he is framed within an archway, as though we have both stepped out of time to look at each other from separate worlds. In the boots that he had always coveted, trousers tucked inside, he is standing at a railway station that was to move him from home forever. There is a confidence in the tilt of the head though his journey, about to begin, was unpredictable. First he made his way to Hamburg where he worked without proper papers, illegally, doing odd jobs, before hiring on to shovel coal on a freighter bound for Montreal by way of Liverpool. In later years, he remembered the heat given off by the boilers and the coal dust embedded in his hands that gave a grey face to the bread passed from stoker to stoker at meal time. He remembered that the freighter was infested with lice that had established a companionship not only with the sailors but with the mattresses they slept on. By the Liverpool docks, my father caught the eye of a peddler and bought a new mattress, the cost to be docked from his wages when the freighter returned to the home port. As soon as the freighter tied up in Montreal, he washed his hands, disembarked as though for a

Uncle Rudolph urging David to leave for Peru.

My father just before leaving Czernowitz.

a casual walk around the harbor, and mounted a #55 streetcar that followed St. Lawrence Boulevard north from the waterfront. The conductor watched as my father ignored the coin box, then followed him to his seat and reached into my father's pocket until he found a coin that satisfied him—it must have been foreign—and snapped it into the coin box. Meanwhile, my father counted the stops until he came to the fourteenth. After stepping down at the corner of Villeneuve, he scanned the nearby buildings until he found the address he had been given when he left home, and knocked on its door. No answer. Before long, a couple out for a stroll, possibly taken by his confused expression, asked him whom he was looking for. He unfolded a sheet of paper with the name of a cousin, Laxer, scrawled across the creases. "They've moved," the couple said. "I'll wait," said my father.

He would not have been buoyant as he waited for his cousin. Thus far the new world had been disappointing. The rows of shops he had just seen as the streetcar trundled north past Sherbrooke, Prince Arthur, Pine, and Rachel, had none of the elegance that he remembered from the broad streets of Hamburg, a bustling commercial center from its Hanseatic days to the present. Even more disappointing were the narrow streets and cramped houses in the old quarter of Quebec City, where the freighter had stopped briefly before tying up in Montreal. The new world was anything but new. The faces of these cities seemed wrinkled, unshaven. Still, there were compensations. After weeks below deck he was on land again, with the name of a cousin clenched in his fist, able to imagine a future. Later, he heard that the freighter on its return voyage to Europe had gone down.

My mother's passage was less dramatic. From their home town of Gora Kalwaria, she and my grandmother traveled by horse and wagon twenty-five miles north to Warsaw. The city's wide streets and the bulge of its public buildings made Gora Kalwaria seem emaciated, thinning even those fulsome memories of the pear and cherry orchards, the trees bowed, heavy with fruit. After one night in Warsaw, a train carried them north, past what she would later remember as only a blur of meadow and spotted cows. In the harbor of Danzig, on September 22, 1923, she boarded the *Orlando*, a 4200 ton hulk, and, along with 500 others, settled in on the 'tween deck, located above the cargo hold and below the first class cabins on the main deck. As the boat nosed its way out of the harbor, and the choppy water of the North Sea built into swells, my mother crouched in her berth, hugging her pillow, fighting off queasiness and worrying about what lay ahead.

After an inch-by-inch passage through the Kaiser-Wilhelm Kanaal, and the renewed swells of the North Sea, especially near the Doggerbank, where the waves thudded more heavily against the sides of the boat, the *Orlando* approached the English coast. My mother should have been relieved, possibly buoyed, at the end of the first leg of her journey, and she would have been but for the waves of fish smells blowing out from Grimsby, and the delay in the estuary of the Humber, waiting for high tide. Finally, at noon on September 25, they disembarked at Hull's Albert Docks. Her mother handed papers to officials and led her through a succession of corridors, and finally onto another train that carried them across an English landscape with bales of hay and dark mounds that reminded my mother of the coal that merchants back in Gora Kalwaria hauled in their wagons. In the darkening afternoon among the stiff-necked chimneys exhaling swirls of black smoke, she sounded out names that were new to her—Leeds, Huddersfield, Manchester—as the train paused at each station.

My mother would remember little from her brief stay in Liverpool—she was too exhausted—only the meal at the Jewish lodging house that reminded her of her mother's cooking. At the port on their day of departure, satchels in hand, mother and daughter were astonished by the looming 16,400 ton *Doric*, which to their eyes looked capable of carrying the entire population of Gora Kalwaria across the Atlantic. Out on the Irish Sea, my mother—sea sick again—retreated to her cabin in the bowels of the ship, from which she ventured on deck only twice, each time staring ahead and

The 16,400-ton *S.S. Doric.*

seeing nothing but the greyness of the western sky. The steward, concerned about his young passenger, brought her daily trays of food to tempt her appetite: broth that nauseated her as it sloshed from side to side in the bowl, carrots, and something leafy green. And also oranges. But now on shore, after seven days on the Atlantic, with the thudding waves, the wet salt air behind her, she marveled at the size of those oranges, the thickness of the rind. She had set them aside, emblems of a life to come.

The immigrants in my neighborhood usually arrived with some scrap of education. What my mother brought was the result of her mother's squirrel-like scrambling after every available opportunity for her daughter. During the fighting in Gora Kalwaria in World War I, the schools shut down, not to open again until after the Armistice. By then, my mother was already eight years old. My grandmother, Baba Rose, felt that her daughter had to make up for lost time. Thus, in addition to public school, Baba Rose sent my mother to French and German tutors and also had a rabbi come to the house so that she could learn Hebrew. In her "nice (public) school with a few rooms," which she distinguished from the town's not-so-nice school with one room that she later attended, both sorties from her otherwise Jewish milieu, she discovered the world as allegory, the good people who comforted, the bad who terrified. Her principal, an icon of goodness, said good-bye when she left in the seventh grade for her voyage across the ocean, even told her what linens to take on the boat. Not like the teacher who wrote nothing on her work, except a zero—an anti-Semite, she thought in retrospect. He was one other part of that hostile world she remembered, soldiers shooting while she cowered in a cellar during the war; thugs beating an old Jewish peddler; or, during holiday services, bullets splintering the walls of the synagogue. In school she learned the rudiments of arithmetic and language, outside of school how to navigate through situations in which she was powerless.

In Montreal's Devonshire elementary school, struggling with a new language, she sat with smaller children, third graders. Soon she had had enough and decided to drop out. The principal, paternal, like the one she remembered in Gora Kalwaria, urged her to stay, drawing her future as he might have done for others—"what are you going to do? Clean floors?" and moved her up to the fifth grade. But at fourteen, with fractured English and fully developed breasts that set her apart from the other girls in the class, she gathered her books and pencils, and for the last time, heard the school door close behind her.

What my father acquired by way of education was little more than an introduction to arithmetic from his brothers, augmented by visits from an itinerant rabbi who, in addition to performing basic ceremonial functions, taught children a smattering of yiddish through a pedagogy of tweaking ears or slapping backs of heads. Even this rudimentary education came to a halt during World War I, but by War's end, he was already aware of gifts unrelated to words and numbers on a page. As a tinsmith apprentice in Czernowitz, pounding nails into sheets of tin roofing, he discovered he could repair anything and that he was attracted to materials, all kinds of materials, things he could surround with his hands, but especially metals. In an old photo album, standing in his work overalls beside his garage on Lagauchetière Street near Peel in downtown Montreal, he is holding the lengthy shaft of a hammer, its head slung over his

Father's first garage on Lagauchetière Street.

shoulder. His other hand, dropped by his side, looks even larger than I remember it when he shook my hand. Over the years he became a master shaper, a Hephaestian who could give form to matter.

Several years ago, as an adult with children of my own, I wanted a share of my father's Hephaestian skill, to be able to shape things as he did, effortlessly, and eventually to pass this knowledge on to my own children. But working with metal as he did raised immediate obstacles. What tools would I need to do the work? What metals would I shape? And to what end? I couldn't imagine the satisfaction that I sought coming from straightening the fenders of automobiles. It all seemed distant from my own inclinations. But working with wood wasn't. I could picture myself building furniture: oak tables, black willow cabinets, maple benches, all finished so that they looked like pieces bought at a department store that I could either keep for myself or give away as gifts.

What I failed to realize was that my father's relationship to metal was special, more a gift than a skill, as though he and the metal he shaped had a private language which only he could hear and understand. For me the wood was merely wood, speechless and inert. True, I could appreciate how hours of devoted sanding with paper that ran from a rough 36 grit to a fine 400 grit would raise a hardwood grain to prominence, but it never spoke to me, or, if it did, I never heard. I stayed with the craft for a few years, making pieces that I still use, but I never saw myself in a workshop as anything more than a plodder.

After my mother dropped out of school, she earned her living as a seamstress. In her first job, sewing linings into garments in a factory, she heard her work praised repeatedly. Now she would no longer have to endure the humiliations of a Devonshire classroom. Years later she would brag, "I earned as much as a man." Like my father, she had acquired the confidence that comes from the ends of one's fingers, their agility convincing her again and again that they could do anything.

Aside from recollections about her job, she rarely spoke about that period of her life between quitting school and marrying. Only a photo or two from that time have been preserved in the family album. In one, she poses on the stage of the Monument National Theater as a gypsy, her left hand on her waist, her right holding a tambourine—a ribbon suspended from it—over her head. The stage is elaborate with a parquet floor and a staircase made for grand descents. In this photo, taken in her late teens, there is already a disposition to the plumpness which she refused to accept, marshalling against it a variety of diets which she resolved to follow, but broke with only limp attempts at rationalization. Nevertheless she is self-assured, as if she has suddenly discovered the satisfaction in an audience's applause.

Still, I remain puzzled by my mother's appearance on the stage of the Monument National. Among the theaters that featured Yiddish

Mother on the Monument National stage.

plays and other entertainment, the Monument National was the pres-
tigious venue chosen by visiting companies from New York, the most
popular of which was Maurice Schwartz's troupe. Jewish immigrants
who spent much of their time in the drabness of textile factories hun-
gered for the success of these celebrities, whom they imagined sipping
wine in luxurious restaurants and wearing fashionable clothes. But to
the children of those immigrants, including myself, the Monument
National and Yiddish theatre meant nothing, and by the time I appreciated the luster and rich colors of Maurice Schwartz's posters pasted
on walls along St. Lawrence Boulevard, they had begun to fade. Yiddish theatre was disappearing, giving way to cinema. Immigrant Jews
no longer depended on the comfort that Yiddish theater provided;

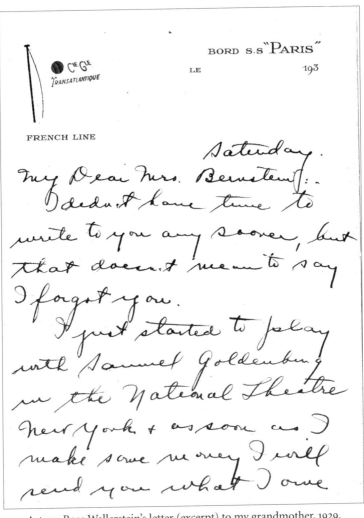

Saturday.

My Dear Mrs. Bernstein: — I didn't have time to write to you any sooner, but that doesn't mean to say I forgot you.

I just started to play with Samuel Goldenburg in the National Theatre New York & as soon as I make some money I will send you what I owe

Actress Rose Wallerstein's letter (excerpt) to my grandmother, 1929.

they were ready to loosen their ties to their homelands in favor of the westernized fantasies provided by Hollywood.

What was it that ushered my mother onto the Monument National's stage during its most popular period? True, her voice was pleasing when she took it into song, but she could have been replaced by many others with equally pleasing voices. The beginnings of an explanation may lie in a letter written on *SS Paris* stationery by the actress Rose Wallerstein. In it she thanks my grandmother for taking late payment on a gown. The letter was written in 1929, at a time when my mother occasionally performed on stage in the evening, but during the daytime worked with her mother, whose customers included several of the Monument National's actresses, among them, Rose Wallerstein. Were my mother's turns on stage the reward for an added frill to a gown, a discounted dress, or was Rose Wallerstein taken by some Yiddish melody my mother happened to be humming, a pin in her mouth, as my grandmother circled the half-finished garment with a chunk of marking chalk in her hand? Or, after all, was she taken by my mother's voice as I would be in later years?

Contours of the Neighborhood

THE THREE STORY HOUSES still squat in their places. No longer swelling with immigrants who bombarded the street with Yiddish accents, they still stare inscrutably at one another, even as they are being disemboweled to make room for the interiors that professionals consider more chic. I assume these new owners are as captivated as I am by the facades, grey limestone and various tones of brick rising to pressed metal cornices, parapets and mansards that crown the row houses, the mansards hinting at the pomp of Louis Napoleon's Second Empire. They would not have been captivated by the old heating systems. Seventy years ago, when my parents unpacked their belongings first at 4175 Clark Street and four years later across the street at 4112, these systems were as primitive as when originally installed during the first decade of the twentieth century. I remember cairns of coal heaped high in the cellar and rats scurrying for an exit between the coughs of the furnace. Even rodents insisted on a threshold of comfort.

The outside stairways rising steeply from the street to the second story are unique, and part of their charm is that they spit in the face of Montreal winters. An architectural historian claims that they were built for reasons of economy and space. Every square foot of these flats was precious, and it was cheaper to build an outside stairway, shared by the occupants of the two upper flats, than an inside one. Not as charming an explanation as the one, probably apocryphal, that views them, exposed to public view, as a means to discourage teenage necking. Whatever their purpose, these stairways are a visual delight, at least for three seasons of the year; but on icy winter mornings, whether they cut a straight swath or swirl down to the sidewalks, they are hazardous. In one of my earliest memories, my father, having slipped, is sliding down a flight of those stairs, bump by bump, holding me tightly to spare me the shock, while I laugh uproariously.

As I drive along Clark Street, a truck backs out of a lane I once crossed on my way to school. A mother wheels a double carriage past the lumber yard wall that I used to spray with sponge balls. I park and look down one end of the street, then the other, but look for what? A man and his teen age son gesture animatedly, speaking a language that is neither English nor French. Nor is it Jewish. Are they Greek? Portuguese? I sniff pointlessly for the clannishness of my childhood neighborhood, which often felt like a small Jewish tug in a harbor with a hulking English man of war on one side of it and a French on the other. We were an "us," living in a world dominated by "them."

As a child, it never occurred to me that our neighborhood had not always been as it was. But, in fact, we Jews were relative newcomers, not only to Montreal, but to all of Canada. Cardinal Richelieu's edict in 1627 prohibiting non-Catholics from settling in New France was aimed at Huguenots, but had the effect of excluding Jews as well. Even Abraham Gradis, the wealthy shipbuilder from Bordeaux. Although his timely deliveries of provisions in the 1740s and 50s saved the French garrison in New France, he was not permitted to set foot on shore. Possibly some Jews may have avoided detection and slipped in. We know of at least one, Esther Brandeau, who managed it in 1738, disguised as a cabin boy. When her identity was discovered, the authorities decided that, rather than deporting her, they would convert her to Catholicism. For a year she parried the questions of the nuns, saying just enough to raise their hopes but never actually repudiating her faith. Finally, the colony's chief administrator lost patience. Esther was returned to France, leaving behind only a residue of questions. What had brought her to New France in the first place? Had she felt trapped in the Sephardic enclave of St. Esprit in her native France? Had she longed for a young man who had settled in the new colony? Was she, like the Jews of Eastern Europe in the following century, looking for a better life? Or had she simply been taken by the pageantry of ships sailing north along some river into the English Channel and from there out toward the darkening sky?

On the British side a different policy toward Jews prevailed. A number of Jewish officers in General James Wolfe's army arrived with him from England and, in 1759, helped defeat the French on the Plains of Abraham. With the British conquest of Canada secured, many of these officers resigned their commissions and stayed on as civilians. From the beginning, they were allowed to practice their faith, thanks to the guarantees included in the Plantation Act passed by Parliament in 1740 which encouraged Jews and dissenters to emigrate to the colonies. By 1777, Canada's first synagogue had been established on Montreal's Notre Dame Street near the current court house.

Even so, Jews were denied the full rights of citizenship; they could not, for instance, serve in the colonial legislature since it required its members to swear an oath of allegiance on "the true faith of a Christian." Thus, Ezekiel Hart, whose father had served under Wolfe, though duly elected on two occasions as representative for Trois-Rivières, was prevented from taking his seat. He did, however, live to see Jews granted the rights and privileges enjoyed by other citizens in Quebec in 1831, followed by full rights as British subjects in the following year.

By the end of the nineteenth century Jewish names appear prominently in the professions and commerce: Aaron Hart, dean of the medical school at Bishop's University; Jules Helbronner, the editor-in-chief of *La Presse*, Henry Joseph, the first to build and charter ships for transatlantic trade; Jacob Henry, instrumental in establishing the Newfoundland Telegraph Company's first wireless link between England and Canada; Jesse Joseph, president of the Montreal Gas Company, founder of the Montreal Telegraph Company, and the first steamship line between Canada and Belgium. Members of a still miniscule Jewish population, these men mixed freely with their non-Jewish business associates and shared their lives of affluence. Clearly, other than religion, they had little in common with the hordes of Eastern European Jews funneled onto the shores of Canada between 1885 and 1925. To the established Jews of Westmount, the new immigrants clinging to the tatters of their lives were not merely a pitiful sight, they were an embarrassment.

The newcomers—my parents among them—settled on either side of St Lawrence Boulevard, still commonly known as the Main, in the western section of what is now called the Plateau Mont-Royal, a borough that unfolds from the eastern slope of Mount Royal into a flatness stretching from Sherbrooke Street north to the Canadian Pacific Railway track at Van Horne, and from Hutchinson Street east to the track near d'Iberville. But while flatness describes the topography of the neighborhood, it does not reflect its active temper either now or in its early days. In the late 1890s, a generation before my parents moved into our first house on Clark Street, a Montreal carter trundling with horse and wagon north along St. Lawrence Boulevard, would have witnessed hectic development. St. Lawrence, which bisects the city into eastern and western sectors, was then a shamble of rollers, wheelbarrows, workmen, bricks, scaffolding, noise, dust, and a succession of deep holes with ladders protruding like the stretched necks of giraffes. Sewer lines and water pipes had been laid a few years earlier, but now it was time to pave the street, add streetcar rails, and install new sidewalks. Houses and shops were being razed to widen the street even though parts of it had been completed only fifteen years earlier. As the carter's wagon passed the intersection of Duluth, then Rachel, then Marie-Anne, he would have noticed a density of row houses to the east as far as he could see, mostly two stories high, many built of brick and some, more costly, of stone. But if our carter looked westward to the slant of the sun, he would have seen a number of still empty lots through which he could glimpse the greenery of Mount Royal a few blocks away, especially if he came by on a Sunday when the work crews were idle and the construction dust had settled. Beyond the intersection of St. Lawrence Boulevard and Mount Royal Avenue was the suburban town of St. Louis, where the neighborhood thinned out, even to the east, but, again, especially to the west, where houses were now separated by vast, open spaces that seemed to be waiting for something to happen. And something did. During the first decade of the twentieth century those spaces, with their weeds and patches of tall grass, would be filled in with solid lines of triplexes that ran from one end of a cross street to the other, their density broken occasionally by narrow lanes that peddlers drove down, hawking their wares. By 1910, the Town of St. Louis lost its autonomy and became yet another ward of the City of Montreal.

When our carter got as far as the intersection of St. Joseph Street, he might have paused to watch stone masons working on the new portico of the church of Saint Enfant-Jesus. Now he was actually in Mile End, a village not incorporated into Montreal until 1910. He might well have continued for another mile to the Pacific Railway Depot although between the church and station there were only scattered buildings set among woods and empty spaces.

But he would have seen enough activity along his route to know that the residential neighborhoods on both sides of the Main were undergoing transformation. By the beginning of World War I almost all of the empty spaces had been filled in. The row houses that went up, built primarily as speculative ventures, allowed the owner to live on one floor and rent out the other flats. The fact that most Montreal row houses of the early twentieth century looked alike is due to the building codes of the day, which directed the builder's attention to new considerations of comfort, health and aesthetics, and, as a result, changed the faces of housing in the area. Unlike many late nineteenth century row houses, including those found east of St. Lawrence Boulevard, the early twentieth century row houses were to be built to certain dimensions and to be fronted by façades of either high-quality brick or limestone. Windows had to be in a specified proportion to the rooms they looked out of, resulting in houses with more daylight and improved natural ventilation. Indoor bathrooms were mandatory. Streets were wider and lit with lamps, and paved sidewalks replaced wooden ones. Façades, now rising to a third story, were set back further from the street, an arrangement which permitted a front stairway and a garden where at least one family could plant flowers, vegetables, perhaps a tree.

I grew up in one of those houses. Like every other house in the neighborhood, it was built on a lot that had been carved out of several nineteenth-century properties owned by one Stanley Bagg, Esquire. That property, which was gradually divided and sold off by his son, Stanley Clark Bagg, and his grandson, Robert Stanley Bagg, had become a good part of Montreal's Jewish district by the early twentieth century.

Our house sat on Clark Street, named in memory of Stanley Clark Bagg's mother, whose maiden name was Clark. But, curiously enough, a 1907 map shows that it used to be called Mitcheson, the family name of his wife. One can only wonder why the one woman was supplanted by the other. The name "Bagg" had been memorialized as far back as the 1850s in the name given to a street that ran parallel to Sherbrooke. But at the end of the century that street was swallowed by another. Within a few years, as if to make amends, a new Bagg Street was created. He would not have been flattered. The newly constructed street that would ever bear his name was a stunted run of standard Montreal triplexes.

We were the seventeenth occupants of the flat at 4175 Clark Street. From L. Cohen, a tailor, the second occupant, to our immediate predecessor, Max Kingstone, a painter, the flat sheltered immigrant tradesmen, primarily garment workers. By the time we settled there in 1938, the street had changed its ethnic mix. In 1891, when Clark ran a mere two blocks from Duluth to Marie-Anne and was home to only thirty families, the ratio of French residents to English was three to one. But Jews were already beginning to move in. *Lovell's Montreal Directory* that year lists H. Blum, tailor; Abraham Goldstein, owner of Montreal Feather; and Saul Vineberg, manager of H. Vineberg & Co. By 1924 the trickle had become a torrent; with the exception of a few families, this stretch of Clark had become exclusively Jewish.

We were the seventeenth occupants of the flat at 4175 Clark Street.

These immigrants from Eastern Europe had moved slowly northward from the neighborhoods that straddled the Main below Sherbrooke Street into the area circumscribed by St. Denis on the east, Park Avenue on the west, Mount Royal Avenue on the north, and Sherbrooke Street on the south.

My parents first moved into the area in 1930, at 3631 Colonial Avenue, before settling into our ground-floor flat on Clark. On one side of our front door an arched way led into a yard that may once have been used for stabling horses. By the time my family arrived, it contained little outside of broken glass, weeds, burdock, and rats that congregated there in groups large enough to be intimidating, though they seemed comfortable with one another, like members of a family lounging after Sunday dinner. We didn't play much in that yard. The only time I recall spending there was when our upstairs neighbors, an orthodox family, built a Sukkah for *Succoth*, the harvest festival. On those occasions, the rats, perhaps responding to the fierce red beard of the descending patriarch, moved discreetly to

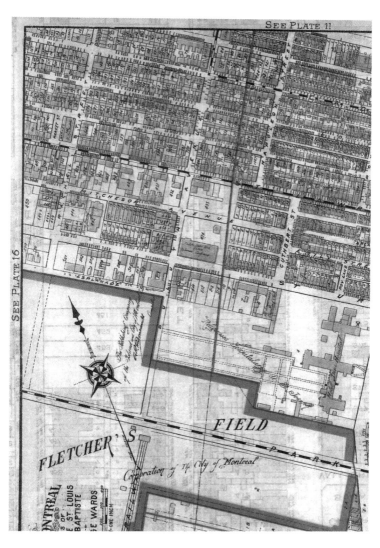

A.R. Pinsoneault, *Atlas of the Island and City of Montreal and Ile Bizard*, 1907.

the edges of the yard and stayed there until the Sukkah disappeared and they could reestablish their tenancy.

Despite the rats, who seemed to have a clear sense as to where their turf ended and where human tenancy began, I never considered Clark or its neighboring streets to be a slum and bristle at, or at least question, this characterization that Judith Seidl applies in her 1939 study of Montreal's Jews. She does add that the houses west of St. Lawrence (including those my family lived in) "present a more prosperous appearance than east of it." Possibly they did although one of my Clark Street neighbors squeezed a family of five into two rooms on a third floor, the daughter bathing in a neighbor's tub. Still, though the incomes of the neighboring Jews were thin, the unperturbed exteriors of their houses, the unlittered streets, and the occasional tree did not conjure up poverty. And to the eyes of a child, the ornate metal cornices, false mansards, carved wooden balcony supports, mass produced though they were, gave to those exteriors a magical and somewhat elegant quality.

In the neighborhood, anonymity was impossible. We knew the people up and down the street as well as my parents knew the neighbors in their old shetls. On summer nights, when heat lingered indoors, the neighbors chatted on their front porches, exchanging tidbits of gossip over the railings. Whose daughter was marrying a doctor from "the States," whose son had been accepted to McGill's Law School, how the elderly lady across the street was doing with her arthritis. As children, we drifted with equal casualness into one another's homes, observing the mannerisms and sampling the cuisine of those who came from different regions of Europe. I remember one friend's father slicing the fat off of boiled beef and swallowing chunks at a time as though determined to get his share of a rare delicacy.

The houses bulged with children, and in the winter most of us played street hockey, sliding with clumsy overshoes over ice and packed snow. In summer we shifted from game to game under the watchful eyes of our parents. Their accents, sculpted by their origins

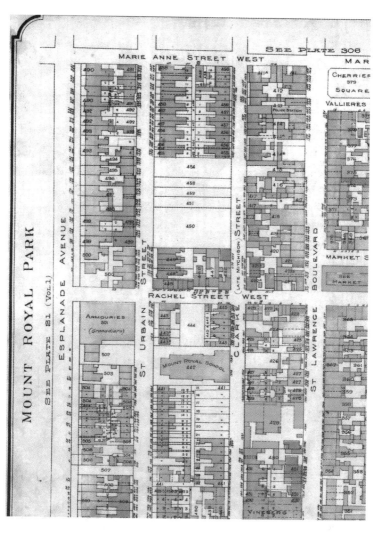

Chas. E. Goad, *Atlas of the City of Montreal and Vicinity*, 1912.

in Vilna, Warsaw, Kiev barely reached the streets before they were overcome by the ponk of sponge balls bouncing off the lumber yard wall and the thwack of the skipping rope on the pavement that accompanied the street songs the girls sang.

We brought a sponge ball to our own special version of hide and seek, "stando," so called because while one boy tossed a ball against the lumber yard wall, the rest of us froze, waiting to hear which of our names he'd call. The boy whose name was called scrambled after the ball while everyone else scattered to hide. As soon as he retrieved the ball, he shouted "stando," and everyone including himself remained where they were. From there he would aim at an exposed haunch, shoulder, whatever was not sheltered by a lamp post or spiraling staircase. Anyone hit was "out." With an arched glance of dismissal, the girls chatted, paying little attention to our athletic flourishes.

We all belonged to one larger clan. We were Jewish, descended from those families that had migrated from Poland, the Soviet Union, and the Baltic states in the twenties and, as a result, had escaped the calamity that was to strike Eastern Europe and the relatives they left behind. Towards the lower end of Clark Street, only one French-Canadian family with three children broke the homogeneity of the street. Although we rarely saw the children, the very idea of them was a threat that constrained us, wielding a power like that of the troll over the Billy Goats Gruff in Grimms' fairy tale. Our liberation came unplanned as it did for the goats. As we made our way to Jewish school one late afternoon, one of the children ran out of his doorway to chase us. My brother turned suddenly, stood his ground, and held a fist out, which our terrorizer, slipping on the ice, obligingly ran into. We were never afraid after that.

Our block ended without ceremony at Duluth Street in a small nondescript general store that no one, including the proprietor, ever seemed to go into or come out of. But I do remember him, a lean and thin-lipped melancholic figure, wrapped in his black and white prayer shawl in the synagogue so that only his face appeared, as though his body had been surrendered to God. As the sun descended on the starred glass of the synagogue, intoning in a voice that could be heard above all others, his body convulsed with prayer.

At the other end of my block, Rachel Street was wider and more interesting than Duluth. Things big and small happened there—my first haircut at Dave's Barber Shop; a parade, menacing in retrospect, of the fascist Bloc Populaire marching through the heart of the Jewish district to protest Canadian participation in World War II, which they viewed as an intrigue of Anglo adventurism financed by international Jewry. Essentially, Rachel Street was the estuary that led to a larger world. And so we preferred to walk in that direction. Even the corner store there was interesting. Nathan—we named the shop for him—would dispense cherry cokes, not from a bottle, but from a hose that fizzed soda into glasses with enormous openings, which we would gulp down with accompanying toasted buns, two for a nickel, stuffed with chips and a dab of mustard. A nickel would buy a hot dog, but with the doors closed in winter, the accumulating aromas from the grill made it possible for us to imagine a hot dog within the bun without spending another penny. The more children that crowded into the shop the wider the smile on Nathan's spherical face extended, as though reaching for the ears flattened against that smiling globe. In his paroxysms of joy, he occasionally reached under the counter for a copy of some muckraking newspaper. Nathan was taking a chance. Possession of such material was risky during Premier Maurice Duplessis' dictatorial stewardship of the province with its notorious Padlock Law that threatened to close any premises containing subversive literature. Only later did I realize that the enclave I lived in was Canada's political hotspot, the only district that sent a communist, Fred Rose, to the House of Commons, not once but twice. Part of Rose's attraction was that the communist party was seen by Rose's Jewish constituents as taking its marching orders from Moscow, and though most of them were not communists, they had working class sympathies as well as admiration for the power that had held its own in the struggle against

Nazi Germany. Still, I didn't linger on Rachel. Rather than an end in itself, it was my gateway to St. Lawrence Boulevard where my mother sent me whenever she needed supplies for her seamstress work at home. On those occasions, I would take her scribbled note past Dave's Barber shop and Labow's Drug Store with its dark ornate cabinetry, a relic of an earlier century, before turning the corner to Katz's Button Shop at 4152 St. Lawrence. The owner, Mrs. Katz, would greet me and, with a smile twisted by some childhood disease, smooth out the note that I had scrunched. I would jog home with the spools of thread that my mother needed to fashion into dresses for women that came to her workshop in the front room. But St. Lawrence was more than a pilgrimage for buttons and thread; it was my introduction to megalopolis, where Jewish and non-Jewish worlds opened their shop fronts along the same wide street with tram tracks running the length of the city. Across the street from Katz's button shop was Sinclair's. Since all I ever saw when I peered through its large framed window were neatly arranged floor model radios, their brand names, Philco and Westinghouse, along with the sign, "Sinclair Radio Co Ltd" became my representation of the Anglo world. In that shop and in Gordon's vacuum cleaner and bicycle shop, I saw uncluttered floors, polished surfaces, antiseptic, yet impressive in the gleam that rose to the window fronts to announce a presence that was not merely local. "Wider still and wider shall thy bounds be set" runs the patriotic song still played on ceremonial occasions in Great Britain. Sinclair and Gordon were its emissaries on St. Lawrence Boulevard. They were more than the *goyim* our elders snickered at. They could establish a presence anywhere, and, we discovered, they did.

In the string of shops, restaurants, and clothing factories along St. Lawrence, immigrants from Eastern Europe spent their working days. Horn's and Lester's, restaurant-delicatessens that served them lunches, also served as forums for literary and political discussions. But the shop that most graphically represented the Jewish immigrant presence was Panyemoshku. Crowds that one might

St. Lawrence Boulevard early 1950s.
Courtesy of André Vigneau, Societé de transport de Montréal.

have seen on market days in Lodz, Lublin, or Vilna leaned against the counters displaying kimmel breads, tubes of salami, and knishes, that would transport them, at least briefly, across the Atlantic to their cities of origin. But more prominent by aroma and size were two prodigious barrels, one containing dill pickles, the other pickled herring. I enjoyed the first, and welcomed the reminder of that pleasure whenever I opened the door. But the chunks of herring emerging like boulders in their opaque sauces, revolted me. It was years before I made my peace with them. Now Panyemoshku is gone along with those who made it their ethnic outpost in Montreal. Still, I cannot walk down St. Lawrence without seeing once again that sign and doorway that led to the shtetls of the East with its barrels of herring and pickles and the sawdusted wooden floor.

While I clung to my rectangular portion of Montreal, I left occasionally to visit aunts, cousins, grandmother, sometimes venturing beyond to other places that mattered for us—a synagogue a couple of blocks away, the Hollywood movie theater, the Rachel Street pool room and the mountain, even Delorimier Stadium where in 1946 my brother and I witnessed Jackie Robinson breaking into professional baseball with the Montreal Royals. He was as much a spectacle for us, citizens of a Montreal within Montreal, as he was for the larger world. Even more so. Like us, wasn't he an outsider? Sprinting around second base to stretch a double into a triple, he made that outside world take notice. One Sunday, a year before Robinson's Montreal debut, my brother and I took the Ontario Street tram, got off at de Lorimier and walked with the throng, a smaller one than usual that Sunday, to park ourselves in the bleachers, the best place to watch an ordinary fly ball reaching for the high wall in right field, only 292 feet away from home plate. Rumor had it that on a windy day, a bunt could find its way to the wall and end up as a double. For some reason, the brightness of the sun, the cast of the shadows, the ball players all seemed a shade darker. I noticed it. So did my brother. And we commented to one another—"Doesn't Roland Gladu, (our neighboring right fielder) seem sunburned?"… "And Red Durrett?" (opposite in left field) and and all through the lineup as we gradually became aware of a muttering

Jackie Robinson.

from the neighboring seats and then realized that ours were the only white faces in the crowd. We hadn't known that our team, the Montreal Royals, was playing in Syracuse that day and that we were watching two teams from the Negro League that had rented the stadium for the afternoon. But one thing was clear enough—there was no diminished quality in the game on the field. The exploits of players such as Duke Snider and Johnny Podres who played with the Montreal Royals before being promoted to the Brooklyn Dodgers still remain with me, but no less vivid is the memory of those players from the Negro League, unacknowledged to devotees of professional baseball and even now occupying only token corners of baseball's Hall of Fame. That afternoon they pitched the ball as it was supposed to be pitched, batted the way we had seen it done on other days, and without squandering a step, sprinted towards balls hit to the outfield, ending their downward arch with a plunk in a leather glove. There was a place for others in the world.

Like other plateaus, the district of St. Louis is topographically flat, at least to the eye, so that from almost any point in that expanse one can see what Cartier first saw from his ship in 1534, something he might have described in his log as a hillock. We make greater claims for it. To us it is "the mountain," overlooking Fletcher's Field, the green area we came to when we walked west to St. Urbain, then to Esplanade, where my father had his first bachelor quarters. At its base Fletcher's Field is broad, extending the width of three city blocks. As a child, I took uninhabited space for granted, assuming that some force of nature had created those expanses to balance the cluttered swells of cities.

On Sundays my father walked there with us, sometimes with a soccer ball which he would kick by swinging his lower leg backwards like a mule, sending the ball over distances that to bug-eyed children seemed infinite. But, while some immigrant families picnicked on Fletcher's Field, my parents preferred another open area, with tall grass along Pie IX Boulevard at the eastern extremity of the city. Here, opposite a stand that sold *chiens chauds*, we would spread our blankets and peel the hard boiled eggs that accompanied my mother's thickly stuffed salmon salad sandwiches. The hours stretched as we rolled in the grass or hid from our parents while bees flitted from corn flower to corn flower. At sunset we drove home listening to what the golden age of radio offered—Henry Aldrich, Jack Benny, and Edgar Bergen, welcome guests who joined us each Sunday. Week after week, well into October, when dropping temperatures ended our picnics, we laughed at antics that eventually became as predictable as Charlie McCarthy's quips on attractive women, whose warmth his wooden hands would never feel, all part of a world shaded by the palm trees of Beverly Hills, far removed from my father's 1940 Chevy and those barrels at Panyemoshku where flotillas of dill pickles and pickled herrings proclaimed their citizenship.

When I was a child, it was possible to reach the summit of Mount Royal on an open-air tram which wound its way to the lookout, under which the city spread out like a topographical map, along the St. Lawrence River, beyond the Jacques Cartier Bridge to the east, as far as the oil storage containers. The mountain was more a symbol than a place of play though in the winter it provided enough slope for us to work up a spurt of speed on a sled with steel runners or on a toboggan with two or three of us clinging to its thin padding. Plastic spheres that have since driven these vehicles into museums did not exist. We would not have known what to do with them, too large to throw, too small to lie on. From the lookout, the city was vast; its twinkling eyes acknowledged the possibility of hurtling ourselves through braids of darkness into whatever possibilities we could find down there. To a child about to step into his teens, the choices were both limited and large.

Barbers

WHEN WILLIAM THE GOOD, Archbishop of Rouen, prohibited the wearing of beards in 1096, it was not the first time that attention focused on the power of the barbering profession and the snipping of hair. Hair did more than make the man. It was once seen as the means by which good and evil spirits both entered and exited the body. And, therefore, those with the skill to direct this metaphysical traffic by arranging, trimming, and tying hair acquired stature. Although by the Middle Ages, the clergy had taken over intercourse with spirits, barbers in Europe still maintained their prestige as professionals, even extending their activity to include surgery and dentistry, much to the chagrin of both surgeons and dentists. To these functions they added another, bloodletting, when the council of Trent constricted the clergy's medical practice in 1163, forbidding them to bleed patients on the grounds that it was sacrilegious for God's ministers to draw human blood. Though barbering has slipped in the general esteem to what it is today, one craft among many, we recognize in Samson, eyeless in Gaza, shorn and deprived of his God-like strength, our own vulnerability. The fleece that we lose when a barber shears us is more than filaments of dead protein; it is a layer of ourselves, a marker of what is to come. We recognize—as Samson does—that we are merely bipedal, featherless, mortals, and we are diminished, both by the recognition and the loss of hair. And in that recognition we become, like Samson, less god-like, more human.

My first haircut would now be considered modish, something like an Iroquois cut, but sixty-five years ago, during World War II, it had political significance. After the dismal British military failures in Norway and Crete, the V-for-victory sign was a common gesture, initially expressing defiance, later celebrating the successes in North Africa and Sicily. Poster after poster featured the triumphal parting of the fingers; and on the Movietone news, Winston Churchill often obliged with a smile of confidence and a cocky display of the sign. In those days there was an epic strut in the air that was hard to avoid. And so, on a sudden impulse, my brother and I and our next door neighbor Shloime decided to join the war effort. Nothing in our houses would do as a weapon. Our imaginations had not leapt to the possibility of a broom serving as a rifle, but we could all flash a V for victory sign. Of course it had to be displayed where it could be seen. The top of the head, we decided. The scissors on my mother's sewing machine became our barbering instrument. We took turns on one another until each of us had a haircut with some semblance of the V-for-victory sign, a landing strip for the eyes of any parent. When my mother returned home with a bag of groceries, she was at a loss as to which landing strip to settle on, my brother's, Shloime's, or mine. That day our V-for-victory patriotism and home barbering ended simultaneously.

Later, when my brother and I first entered Dave's barber shop, we were unafraid; we did not even feel the need to have our mother close at hand, and with a lightness of heart, had left her at her sewing machine. But Dave's hot breath was enough to cow me when I climbed onto the board that he had placed across the arms of his chair, especially when what I saw in the mirror was myself, my shoulders covered with a white smock as though I were presenting my head for surgery.

Dave worked away. And, though the teeth of his clippers chomping at fringes of my hair was mere monotony for those poring through their newspapers, I was riveted by the sight of my curls tumbling to my shoulders, or, if I squirmed, to Dave's tiled floor, where they lay along with the snips of previous clients, until Dave swept them up.

Lighter by a headful of hair, I waited while my brother had his turn. What was left on my head felt strange, uncomfortable. What remained for my brother must have felt even worse, because once released from the swirl of the barber's chair, he grabbed his coat and bolted through the door for home as if to escape whatever else Dave might have in store.

The shearings that followed were never as dramatic, but each visit introduced us to a world that extended beyond our immediate families, a world populated by customers who represented the range of our ghetto: a pants presser from the Vineberg Building, a vendor of live chickens from the nearby Rachel Street market, and the owner of Moishe's steakhouse, flicking the ash from his cigar as he offered twenty-five cents to any youngster willing to surrender his turn on the barber's chair. And then there were the barbers themselves, individuals with their own quirks. We never got to learn Dave's quirks since our first haircut there was also our last. Instead, my brother and I were directed to Gittelman's, a small shop on St. Lawrence near the Hollywood Theater. There the hair got swept up more frequently as the two barbers guided their clippers and scissors along the heads of those who crowded into the shop. Gittelman, whose haircuts were trim and raised no eyebrows, had disconnected himself from his European roots. He could quip and banter with his customers in unaccented English, although he smiled only rarely and only rarely raised his eyes from the head of hair that he was shaping. The owner of the shop, he carried an air of competence, his badge in the New America. Shuster, his employee, was a throwback to a previous page. His haircuts were notorious, as though given by a blind man, with patches of hair cut or uncut according to whim or lack of concentration. He was more interested in telling stories. Customers preferred Gittleman, but more than once, my father, fearing that Shuster's feelings would be hurt if he surrendered his turn in order to wait for the owner, meekly took his place on Shuster's chair. Half an hour later, he would emerge, scarcely recognizable, but with a bevy of stories.

I did whatever I could to avoid Shuster, curling up unobtrusively in the corner where Gittleman worked. But when my father brought home a book that Shuster had written, something printed in Yiddish, "Leibig Foon Amol," (Leibig Once Upon a Time), a memoir of his Polish village, I realized that Shuster had a hidden life: he was an author, writing about a world forever gone. In Jewish script, Shuster had brought across the Atlantic a portrait of his world, with photographs to confirm his claims. His stories rose from that book with each wisp of cut hair. They seemed to be as numerous as the clumps of hair that fell beneath his scissors. So many that they now blur into one continuous narrative about timid girls, boasting adolescents, and young men leaving the shtetls to try their luck in Warsaw, Lodz or even the cities of North America. It no longer mattered that the hair was unevenly cut; he was an author, my father felt, and therefore allowances had to be made. It was then that I learned about the space and indulgence given to those who produced little with their hands, who merely reflected, sometimes on the Europe of their childhood, sometimes on the world, sometimes on religious mystery. Typical of course was the Talmudic scholar who devoted all of his time to ancient Hebrew texts in order to determine what others had said regarding the ways of Providence. But Shuster was something else. He had actually set pen to paper and, rather than drifting from the world, had remained in it, however awkwardly.

When it became too embarrassing to endure his haircuts or, even worse, to humiliate him by maneuvering to get my hair cut by Gittleman, I shifted my patronage to Eddie and Struzer, a shop below my Aunt Faige's flat, to which, after a haircut, I could make my way for a cup of cocoa and a welcoming smile.

Struzer, short and thin, with a surprisingly bald and unbarbered head, was an inveterate cynic given to lewd asides. Squinting, he walked around his chair with a proprietor's confidence, taking a snip here, a snip there, as though he were trying to catch customers unaware and web them into the stains of his mind. At best, I felt uneasy beneath the motion of his scissors and comb, apprehensive about those fingertips hovering above my scalp. I regarded my departure from his chair not merely as a relief, but as a liberation.

The cynicism around one chair extended to the other, over which Eddie puffed out breath from time to time like a creature breaking through the surface of the sea. But Eddie's cynicism, relegated to politics, reflected what most in the neighborhood felt about a government that they saw representing the powerful against the weak. Otherwise, Eddie was a compendium of suggestions about a variety of things, prophetic in some ways, like pointing to the hazards of fatty foods. Fortunately or unfortunately for me, the aroma of my mother's chopped liver, the paté that festooned Jewish holidays, was more compelling than Eddie's advice.

The Holidays

As CHILDREN, WE PAID little attention to Christmas except for the Santa Claus parade that we followed from Aunt Faige's balcony on Villeneuve Street until it swung left on Park Avenue and made its way between the spread of Fletcher's Field and Mount Royal to Eaton's, Montreal's major department store. A few stragglers followed in the wake of the floats, like the last mice after the piper of Hamelin. We didn't stay to watch them disappear. We were more tempted by the welcome that we could count on at Aunt Faige's flat. Typically, as the last stragglers disappeared, she would leave her sewing machine and lead us to the kitchen at the end of a long hall where she poured scalding milk onto heaps of powdered cocoa and slathered butter on slices of kimmel bread.

Like my mother and grandmother, Faige took pride in fashioning dresses for Jewish dowagers. Maneuvering cloth for hour upon hour through the clacking teeth of their machines was not mindless work for these seamstresses, but their means of survival, how they sustained their families, sent their children to school, and wrung overt praise from others for their craftsmanship. The subdued praise they bestowed upon themselves came primarily from their stewardship of their homes, making the sandwiches that their husbands took to work and their children took to school, seeing that their spaces were neat and clean, with no hint of the chaos that they had left on the other side of the Atlantic. Although the male breadwinners were more than mere drones in ghetto hives, it was the women who created the holy ground that drew the family together. Literally so on Jewish holidays.

The spirituality of our holiday meals was not a vague concept, but an actual demonstration of these family matriarchs governing their festive tables like ancient priestesses. The meals on the first two nights of Passover were those we celebrated most, with small amounts of ceremony and great amounts of food. My grandmother

Aunt Faige, Baba Rose, Mother.

presided first. Slightly under five feet, she was in her own way a giant, having brought her daughters to another continent and raised a family in spite of one useless husband who drank and two others who dwarfed her in size but not in command. My family's seders were traditional, featuring a reading of the Haggadah, the recounting of the exodus of the ancient Israelites from Egypt; the tasting of bits of bitter and sweet morsels signifying moments of that journey, and the serving of the Passover meal. My uncle Chuna, the spitting image of Barry Fitzgerald, dashed through the first half of the Haggadah to the delight of all of us, who willingly surrendered piety for food. Our first real tidbit, hard boiled eggs floating in a bowl of salted water, one of the symbolic reminders of the pain of exodus, was anything but painful for me. Against the crunch of matzoh, the eggs were a treat I devoured with gusto not just at the seder, but for the entire week of Passover. After the eggs came a caravan of other dishes. First a chicken broth with knaidls (dumplings), and a kind of pancake, "chrenzlach," which is unknown, even to most Jews from eastern Europe where it originated. If this pancake were reserved for only a subsection of the chosen, I was pleased to be one of them. Plates heaped with beef, either roasted as brisket or boiled, served with mounds of chicken, followed by stewed fruit covered the table from end to end. Remembering the hunger she

59

had experienced in Poland, my grandmother determined that we should all eat until the very act of swallowing became impossible, demonstrating, like Napoleon, that one could be short but still rule like a despot. She patrolled the table, checking the progress of each plate of food. As soon as she saw a plate emptied, she refilled it. To refuse was unthinkable since she would interpret even a polite "no, thank you," not just as a comment on the food itself, but as a rejection of the loving labor that had produced it. We all knew it would be less painful to die from the suffusion of food than to resist. Like everyone else at the table, I was expected to eat platefuls of food though I was by no means her favorite grandchild. She preferred my cousins, older and more likely to succeed in careers that family elders valued—medicine, law, dentistry, or engineering. Once she referred to me as a *langer loksch*, a long noodle, destined in her mind to come to no good end. Had she lived to see me publish as a poet, she would have felt confirmed in her forebodings.

The second night's seder, held at my aunt Faige's Villeneuve Street flat, followed the pattern of the first, and in the process transformed her from a seamstress in her workaday smock hunched over her machine to the figure standing erect, superintending this seder meal as it moved in stages from her kitchen to her dining room. For this one evening she had abandoned the workroom to revive the magic that had passed through the kitchens of her forebears. Even the gefilte fish, which Jewish housewives now buy in jars, she had created from an actual fish, likely pike or whitefish, which spent its last days swimming in her bath tub. When I first saw it darting within its porcelain confines, I was puzzled that my aunt, practical to the nth degree, had chosen this unusual pet. Only later did I realize it would soon reappear, minced into spheres with onions and spices. Every Jewish housewife was expected to produce a credible chicken soup, but successful gefilte fish was a mark of distinction. Another distinction of the Villeneuve Street seder was that my Uncle Chuna, now on his home turf, sped through the first half of the Haggadah text even more rapidly. His words were now totally unintelligible and would have been so, I believe, even to a fluent speaker of Hebrew.

After the prodigious meal, we drifted to corners of the house where we could sink into a couch or bed. My uncle was left to finish the text with far less company than he had had earlier. He didn't seem to mind. His expression during the reading never changed. It was consistently phlegmatic and as predictable as his pace. On only one occasion do I remember a departure. As Passover approached, an enterprising boy in my elementary school class decided to earn money by selling neckties. I chose a blue one that featured a girl with golden hair and one exposed breast with a pink nipple. Thinking to introduce a novelty to the family's Passover aesthetic, I wore it to the seder. No one said anything; even my mother was speechless. But my uncle reacted to the tie as though a ball of gefilte fish had reconstituted itself as an energetic pike, jumped off its plate, and slapped him on the side of the head for no reason whatsoever. He was scarcely able to read a syllable without stammering. His glance whipped from the Haggadah to my tie as though he were following a championship tennis match and was determined not to miss a stroke.

The Haggadah, reminder of earlier hardships, had little meaning for me then. Even afterwards, as the epochs between the Exodus and the Holocaust turned from incomprehensible shreds into a single tapestry of wandering and persecution, the crowded table at Passover with plates shuffling in slow motion to an orchestra of laughter and chatter reminded me not so much of piety as of conviviality, of the essentials of the comic spirit, of the comforts that human beings could bring to one another. Weighted down by seconds of dessert, the pain of exodus slipped under waves of anecdotes about pranks at school and bankruptcies until it lost its place except as a dim irony.

In my old neighborhood, pieties were expressed on the Sabbath, which began at sundown on Friday, as well as on Jewish holidays— and there were many, not all of which my parents and their neighbors celebrated. For instance, only the orthodox Jews above us at 4175 Clark observed the harvest festival, Succoth; and though Channukah, a celebration of the triumph of the Maccabees, seemed an occasion for triumphal meals and exchange of gifts, my parents and their friends ignored it except for bestowing some token like a draidl, a miniscule device that we would spin to discover by the revealed letters what the fates had in store for us ("shlecht" for poor, "gimmel" for good). For my parents, real gift giving would have been a concession to Christmas, a betrayal.

Like most of the children on our street, my brother and I were required to attend services twice during the year, on Rosh Hashanah—the New Year and Yom Kippur—the Day of Atonement. My father never accompanied us. I suspect he had little interest; I also doubt whether he was able to read the Hebrew in the prayers. At funerals he muttered something, likely reproducing phrases that he had heard many times, but whose meaning he did not know. The task of escorting us to the synagogue was left to Mendel, a friend who had left Romania with my father. Because Mendel was slight, he was not able to work his way across the ocean as my father had by feeding coal into a furnace. Instead, he lingered in Hamburg and followed a year later as a cabin boy and became as trusted a friend as my father had, once handing him a signed blank check when my father needed cash to purchase his first garage. On our two special holidays, Mendel strode along Clark Street with my brother on one side, me on the other, crossing first Duluth, then Bagg before we stepped into the Beth Shloime, a smallish synagogue rebuilt from a house in the late 1920s Saturday morning services were held there as well, but since my parents were driven more by convention than by piety, my brother and I were not held to those, and so were able to sleep in late on Saturday morning. But on Rosh Hashanah, dressed in our best, both shirt and tie, we walked to the beat of Mendel's anecdotes of Czernowitz and of his feats as a boxer. We were impressed though somewhat skeptical.

The mood surrounding Rosh Hashanah was buoyant; it was, after all, a celebration of a new year. Life had gone, life was arriving, and we would be there to see it. We were only dimly aware of the darkness overtaking Jews in Germany and Eastern Europe, of the millions of hands grasping for but unable to reach another year. The inside of the synagogue was crowded with those who attended regularly and others, like us, everyone eager to join this celebration. Because there were more worshippers than the synagogue could accommodate, seats were sold for these holidays; but no one I knew managed to sit for the entire two days, and so the synagogue was as crowded outside as it was inside, with groups chattering, laughing, gesturing.

Following Rosh Hashanah by a week was Yom Kippur. We soon became aware that the barometer of levity was dropping. Inside the synagogue, there was a tension, a sorrow. Dudye Tenebaum, the shop owner down the street, swayed back and forth, wailing out his prayers. Those of us who understood nothing of what his words meant absorbed their intimations of sorrow. After a night and a day with neither food nor drink, we felt tired, hungry, and emotionally emptied. From time to time we drifted outside for fresh air and joined knots of people, all formally dressed, chatting in whispers, but with none of the gaiety of a week before. We remained at the synagogue, our throats getting dryer, until the shofar, the ceremonial ram's horn, sounded to end the service. Along with Mendel, my brother and I returned along the familiar aisle of houses on Clark Street, but at Duluth we swung left towards Fletcher's Field to break our fast at a small general store owned by the Berenbaum family. They were *lantzmann*, from the same town as my father and Mendel, and had rented my father a room in their flat at 4051 Esplanade when he first arrived in Montreal. On the shop counter were sweet wine and honey cake to fill the emptiness that we had brought into the shop. There were some smiles, chatter that concerned their grown-up friends rather than us, and after a half hour or so, Mendel ushered us out the door and deposited us where he had found us earlier. We were done for another year.

First Classrooms

ACROSS THE STREET FROM our home at 4175 Clark, Mount Royal Elementary School was a dominating presence. Four stories high, it had bragging rights over the neighboring houses occupied by tradesmen, primarily textile workers, who in their European villages had not seen a building of that height. Inside, the school was less imposing, and on winter days, when steam hissed through the pipes in the dimly lit dark green corridors with pale green stripes, downright depressing. For seven years I climbed its steep wooden stairs and, always reluctantly, walked the curling planks of wooden corridors into classrooms where neighborhood children crowded to learn the multiplication table, French conjugations, and the significance of the Plains of Abraham.

If my first journeys to elementary school and, later, high school were lonely, they were also brief. The first was a few steps across the street, the second, no more than a block away. Nevertheless, they *were* journeys, and as George Orwell's descriptions of his early schooling remind us, journeys into the vulnerability that children feel in a world of unpredictable adults. At Mount Royal, schoolchildren could never be certain about whether a quirk of behavior would summon a grudging smile from a teacher or the long rubber strap that Mr. Anderson, the school principal, brought down forcefully on the palms of children. There was no deliberation, no appeal, and I was never quite sure how seriously the rules were taken by the teachers. Chattering in line, a strappable offence one week, was overlooked the next. We were all Lilliputians in a land of Gullivers, giants who governed by whim and caprice. When we stumble through a multiplication table or stutter through conjugations of French verbs at age eight, or cower at being yanked out of a queue and sent to the principal's office, we come to realize how helpless we are in a world beset by giants.

My neighborhood companions, who might have provided a sense of belonging, were distributed in other grades and classes, nowhere to be seen, except for a glimpse at recess. The territorial map that they constituted for me, glued into memory the way a passage is for a ship's pilot, with Leo Gold on the second floor of the house next to ours, Shloime Laufer below him, the three Shoub children further down the street, Shye across from them, was useless at school. It was a sonar device that failed to register the children in my classes, who were strangers, and for most of my stay at Mount Royal, like shapes in a viscous solution that pass one another in slow motion with neither magnetic attraction nor a hint of recognition. The familiar shouts of my own neighborhood were a fanfare I never heard within the walls of my classroom. There, despite a constant hum of children's chatter, I was anonymous. I knew no one; no one knew me.

And yet my school career had started out happily enough. In kindergarten we sat close to one another on small chairs in a miniature red schoolhouse, cutting out colored shapes, and tacking them

Mount Royal Elementary School was across the school from our house.

them onto the wall. Nothing more was demanded. But the following September, we were uprooted to rooms with blackboards, some with simple arithmetic in thick white chalk, others with sentences of three or four one-syllable words. The long rows of desks at which we sat were bolted to the floor, as if to thwart anyone planning to break into the school in the dead of night, climb four flights of stairs, and abscond with them. The inkwells set in our desk tops were further indications that playtime was over, that colored construction paper would be replaced by wooden pencils, and aimless splotches of paint by columns of additions and subtractions. The silence in the class had the breath of resignation, as though there were a general recognition that the new order was not for a day or a week, even a year, but for as far into the future as we could see.

As I moved with the predictability of dripping water from grade one through grade seven, I was unaware of the Byzantine nature of Montreal's school system. For instance, it had not yet registered on me that the conversations at recess were exclusively in English. And yet I knew French was out there, perhaps only spatterings in my neighborhood, but these built to incomprehensible masses of sound the further afield I wandered. Where did those speakers go to school? Behind which walls did they learn to speak the language that acquired legitimacy for us only when we reached the third grade and repeated its conjugations for thirty minutes four times a week?

About French Catholics we knew little; they were not part of our world. What we concluded about their schools was largely based on ignorance and stoked by rumor. While I never imagined them as having seven heads and eighteen rows of teeth, like creatures in a Medieval etymology, I suspected that they spent their time differently from us, but precisely what they did during their school days I never learned. It was as though the gulf that separated our communities was too wide to see across. Though I still remain bewildered by that enormous gulf that separated our communities into "two solitudes," it was a gulf we regarded as divinely decreed.

I would later discover that a dual system of education existed in Quebec. Canada's founding document, the British North America Act (1867) delegated responsibility for education to the provinces with the stipulation that the school systems of the two dominant groups, Catholics and Protestants, be financed with public money. This arrangement failed to take into account children of other religious faiths, a negligible group in 1867, but soon destined to grow, especially as a result of Jewish immigration. An accommodation was reached. By the 1890s Jewish children were officially accepted into the Protestant School system, and, in return, Jewish property owners were required to pay a portion of their taxes to the Protestant School Board.

The Protestant community was uneasy about the prospect of their children mingling with those of another culture and even more concerned that their children might eventually be taught by Jewish teachers, though such instructors were few, even in districts that were predominantly Jewish. Mount Royal Elementary School, whose students were almost entirely Jewish from 1941 to 1947, the years I attended, had no more than five Jewish teachers. During my years in secondary school, 1947 to 1951, Baron Byng High, where over ninety-five percent of the eleven hundred students were Jewish, employed only three Jewish teachers.

The grudging attitude toward Jews in Protestant schools must have stimulated the movement already underway in the Jewish community to establish separate schools that would nurture a Jewish identity and prevent their children from being assimilated into a Protestant culture. True, most Jews did stay within the Protestant school system and sent their sons to rabbis only to prepare them for their Bar Mitzvahs. But others, seeking to acquaint their children with Jewish history, the Zionist movement, or radical politics settled their children in Jewish Schools, at least for a portion of each school day. But, while many immigrants welcomed these schools as the best way of keeping Jewish culture alive, others viewed them with deep misgivings. To "uptown Jews," David Roskies observes, the establishment of separate schools was a step back to the ghetto, to the superstition and ignorance that uptown Jews had emigrated from. `

Nevertheless, a number of Jewish schools were established. Judith Seidel documents eight in 1924 serving over twelve hundred and fifty students. Separate from the Protestant school system, Jewish schools were also quite distinct from one another in ideology and emphasis. The Talmud Torahs, established at the turn of the twentieth century, focused on Hebrew and sacred texts; the Folks Shule (People's School), which opened its doors in 1913, emphasized Yiddish learning with only a smattering of Hebrew but, unlike the Talmud Torahs, sought to instill a nationalistic rather than a religious identity; the Peretz Shule, established two years earlier, was similar to the Folks Shule in its emphasis on Yiddish, but in politics subordinated the inculcation of Jewish nationalism to socialist ideals; schools run by communists or the Workman's Circle were totally secular and more militantly radical than the Peretz Schools, "primarily interested," according to Judith Seidel, "in the teaching of left-wing doctrine."

By the time I taught English and history to eighth grade students at Herzliah High School on Clanranald Avenue in 1958, Jewish schools were firmly established. An ambitious school, Herzliah crammed both English and Hebrew studies into each school day. An outsider might assume that its expanded curriculum, which allowed little leisure, would leave the pupils weary and drained. But I found them full of energy, sometimes given to obstreperous clowning, with boundless curiosity about the great books of the west. They reveled in Dostoyevski, Flaubert, Neitzsche, and Ibsen and, with skullcaps on their heads and intellectual banditry in their hearts, brought a holiday enthusiasm to a spirited discussion of these writers. On dank November days, when darkness began to draw the curtain down in mid-afternoon, they made the classroom glow.

When I am driven to excavate memories of my own early education, I initially find myself lost in some mid-afternoon, sunlight spreading across a room with a promise that it will go on forever, like the endlessness of wheat fields. Things around me fade; memory itself fades, and I lose all bearings, where I came from, where I am going and why, possibly because I see nothing that anchors me in the distant past, that reminds me of distinctive moments. In an effort to remember, I push aside more recent distractions, images of travel, for example, that are too vivid and that still bubble in memory—a sailing across a stormy Atlantic, crawling through a lava tunnel in Espanola, running from the incoming tide at Frobisher Bay. I do so as an act of faith, knowing that if I am sufficiently patient, receptive, I will eventually drift through these distractions to my Mount Royal past, touch its brick wall and wedge myself back to where I first peered into a classroom and began a map of discovery, a map of myself, now wandering like a blind man through memory in order to reestablish the contours of memory itself.

Yet, it is remarkable how little comes back to me of my seven years at Mount Royal. With only a few exceptions, what I do remember in that opaque light of another age takes the form of textures, vague feelings of loneliness or apprehension, rather than specific images. Nevertheless, a single classmate comes to mind, Lawrence, a boy with blond hair, a Christian. Whether he was too blond or too Christian, my parents did not see him as a fit companion. While the immigrants in our enclave were almost entirely Jewish, some, though also from the villages of Eastern Europe, were not. For our parents, with memories of pogroms, these gentiles carried the taint of the enemy; for us, their offspring were merely other children, except, perhaps, a bit more blond, with straighter hair. But it did not matter whether my classmates were Jewish or Christian; they were strangers and I felt no solidarity with them. The only occasion in which my Jewish spirit reared to full height with my classmates was at Christmas in the fifth grade when Miss Black had us sing Christmas carols. Our voices were weaker, the words less defined than when we sang secular songs such as "Bobby Shaftoe" and "The Blue Bells of Scotland," except that when we came to the last line of "Silent Night," we clearly enunciated it as "Sleep in heavenly piss."

After that, we sang no more Christmas carols in Miss Black's class. Although I have come to enjoy carols and often find myself vocalizing their lyrics each December, I am to this day uncomfortable with the last line of "Silent Night," and prefer concluding it with the German "Schlaff in himlische ruhe."

Like the unremitting drabness of Mount Royal's halls and classrooms, the curriculum had little appeal for me: the succession of numbers with a dash for subtraction, an intersection of vertical and horizontal for addition, an "x" for multiplication, and something equally whimsical for division, I saw as chaos that lined both sides of my passage from grade one through grade seven. And chaotic is what numbers remained, acquiring for me neither the coherence nor magic that they did for others, or the pliability they took on in the hands of my brother who later studied mathematics at Imperial College in London. And so I plodded through problems involving gallons of milk, change from a five dollar bill, or mounds of apples at the market. History, however, had more appeal. Even regional history with striking names like Frontenac (the governor of New France) or Pontiac and Negwagon (Indian chiefs) or exploits like the voyages of its early explorers—Cartier peering from his ship in 1534 at the slope we now call the mountain; the later voyages of Champlain, especially the one in which he was misled by Hurons, Algonquins, and Montagnais into joining a raid on an Iroquois village; the *coureurs de bois*, who managed to penetrate hinterlands, slipping away from their known worlds by canoe. History, the adventure that other subjects were not, lifted me out of familiar surroundings and deposited me in places where people wore strange clothing and spoke strange languages.

Geography, which we learned from a green text, far larger than our other books, because it contained large maps, was another form of exotica with countries represented in bright colors and names that dazzled the tongue—Mombassa, Ulan Bator, Bombay, even our own Shawinigan Falls. Unfortunately, more was expected from us than the repetition of sounds, no matter how lightly they tripped off the tongue. We had to identify their locations, a chore that interested me far less than memorizing the names of exotic places. With the difficulties that beset me in other subjects, I could not afford a disaster in geography, and luckily discovered a strategy that would placate the teacher. On exams, the cities that I could not specifically locate I arbitrarily designated as ports and let it go at that. At first I assumed that ports were always on oceans. Later on, I learned to my delight that cities on rivers or lakes also qualified. It was amazing how often that one magic word "port" turned out to be the correct answer. In any case, for my teacher, that word sufficed; I was never called on to be more specific or to point at spots on a map. My success at avoiding discovery left me with an abiding attraction to land leaning into the sea, to the beginnings of escape. Even the St. Lawrence River, cumbersome and awkward as it flows by Montreal, had a special attraction when the great ocean liners slowly nudged their way out of the harbor and made their way up through the Gulf to open water.

Although geography was painless, it represented one of the few occasions when I was sent to the principal's office. The class had been taken over by a substitute teacher, who spoke with a Scottish accent sufficiently pronounced to suggest that her Anglo culture and my Yiddish culture would never intersect. Moreover, she may have been unaccustomed to a student whose gaze wandered across the ceiling before settling on window panes and staying there. She seemed perplexed by my unresponsiveness, especially when she glanced over my shoulder and witnessed me writing again and again on the inside cover of my geography book the name, "Herb Cain," a professional hockey player. I am still unable to explain why I chose to single him out. He did not even play for my beloved Montreal Canadians, but for the rival Boston Bruins. Nor can I explain why, at nine years old, I was drawn to a name which joined the domestic intonations of "Herb" to the wandering, tormented biblical Cain. Was I blurting out like a foghorn a direction that my fantasies would take? Whenever I feel mildly claustrophobic and look through the travel pages for cruises to anywhere, preferably some uncharted water, with "no captain, no port in mind," or find myself driving along empty streets at three in the morning, I recall that oversized geography text which identified a direction for journeys—all directions.

In addition to my discoveries in history and geography, composition was something I could always count on to deliver me from the feeling that I was living in an eternally grey November day. I had begun to write brief narratives in which a character awakens after a traumatic experience only to discover that he has been dreaming. I can only speculate as to why I should have fastened onto this pattern, though fasten I did, perhaps because after two or three attempts, the narrative was easy to produce and the teachers appreciated it. Suddenly, I acquired status, and, for the first time, an audience as the teacher required the other children to listen while I read. As I stood at the head of the class, I may have looked sedate, but, inwardly I was grinning from ear to ear. The only other time I had the stage was in a fourth grade puppet show in which I read the part of the puppet Buttercup, but since the audience could not see me and the words were not my own, that moment of triumph was less gratifying. The dismal report cards of my early years might have caused me to languish into total indifference. They didn't. Those dream narratives had given me an oasis filled with servants who served up nothing but praise.

But, at best, getting out of bed and onto the cold floor on school days was something I did grudgingly, especially when I woke to a crust of frost on the window pane. One inducement, though, was to see my father before he left for work. His was a comfort that could raise me from the ground with laughter, off-key singing, and, on weekends, his famous oatmeal. After he left for work, I gave myself the luxury of another fifteen minutes under the covers, dreading the cold outside.

The years from 1940 to 1947 stand like gateways, each one guarded by a teacher whose name still remains in memory although some of the faces have dimmed. I can no longer, for example, remember Miss Davis my first grade teacher. She seems part of an anonymous mass of grade oneishness, as undistinguishable as my fellow students. But one of her lessons took hold. She carefully explained that if one's clothes caught fire, the best course of action was to wrap oneself in a blanket. I misunderstood. A few days later, when someone built a fire on the sidewalk, I threw my sweater into the building flames. Although one of the older boys quickly plucked it out, the stamp of my misdeed was there. The wool, scorched in one or two places, had an unmistakable smoky aroma that could not be attributed to normal wear, nor was I ever able to explain satisfactorily to my mother the scientific principles that had guided my action.

Other teachers leading me on to master language, mathematics, history, geography and penmanship followed in succession, like piano keys: Miss Kayzer, Miss Kastner, Miss Harris, Miss Black, Miss Lifschitz, and Miss Levy. All misses. The only man in the school was the principal, Mr. Anderson. Like a giant in a Grimm's tale he was able to cross a room in two or three strides. Invariably, he had a strap at his side and always seemed eager to use it impulsively, although he usually saved it for more formal occasions when a teacher sent him a recalcitrant student. "Down to the office" was a phrase that had the ring of death. Once out of a teacher's mouth, it leapt into the mind as a picture of pain with red welts on both hands. Mr. Anderson had only to look at you with those stern eyes set beneath forested eyebrows to stiffen you into a paralysis. Liberation came one day when two older boys with no academic expectations strolled into his office and proceeded to pummel him. Afterwards, the boys disappeared from school. Though he had been bloodied, Mr Anderson's cruelty did not diminish, but his stature as a monster did. He had become one of us, depressingly human.

In those classrooms I always felt vulnerable. I was among the smaller children, not gaining inches until well into secondary school. Nothing cushioned me from the sternness of that school except my daydreams.

Having little schooling themselves, my parents resigned all that occurred during the day to the school's discretion, never questioning a teacher's judgment or even inquiring about my progress. But on one occasion they were summoned to the school. It was Edith Mandel's fault. She sat in front of me, her braids falling on my desk, tantalizingly close to my recessed ink well. I could not resist the temptation to tint them a luminous blue. I soon learned that Edith had no appreciation of hair colored blue like that of our comic book heroes, Tarzan and Captain Marvel, because she immediately ran up to the teacher and pointed her finger at me. As a result, I was suspended for a day and my parents had to appear for my reinstatement. Dressed in his auto shop clothes, my father looked properly grave as did my mother. They could not understand how someone with opportunities they never had would give himself to that kind of antic.

Such antics were rare. My day at school normally began with the practice of self-restraint, climbing from the basement with its concrete floors and painted brick walls and smell of urine to the upper floors of classrooms. Hardly uplifting, it required all that schoolchildren could muster to carry it off with an acceptable dignity. Upstairs our teachers exercised the authority of parents—you had to do what they said—backed finally by the stern striding image of Mr. Anderson at full gallop. Of my early teachers, only my third grade teacher Miss Kastner remains three-dimensional, with a broad face more given to smiles than scowls, full hipped with breasts that distinguished her from any of the girls in the room. On rare occasions, she came into my third grade classroom like a grim shadow, throwing out questions that required a knowledge of the multiplication table. A wrong answer was followed by an order to extend an opened hand, which she promptly whacked with a ruler. The pain was temporary; but the humiliation lingered for Miss Kastner was the gateway to our knowledge of women. If the tree in the Garden of Eden was Adam's introduction to sexuality, Miss Kastner was a flowering branch. With chalk marks on the blackboard and her skirt, she ranged to all parts of the room, carrying the messiness of education with energy and passion. Yet, there

Boys and girls of my seventh-grade class at Mount Royal Elementary, 1947.

was a softness to her, a fullness that was warm and engulfing. With no awareness of women's anatomy, we felt that there was something in her that was completing and coupling, though how or what remained mysteries. My last two teachers at Mount Royal, who saw me as quirky, given to daydreams, and generally unresponsive were serious to the point of being ponderous. When I was aware of them, it was not in the way I saw Miss Kastner. The very sight of them evoked vague images of the Canadian north, acres and acres of frozen tundra.

My last memory of Mount Royal is a pair of photographs our seventh grade class posed for in the concrete schoolyard, one of the boys, another of the girls. On first glance, the pictures seem like typical school leaving photos, several pupils with arms around each other and on their faces a variety of expressions, suggesting that some were looking forward to leaving, but others leaving with apprehension. In the photo of the boys' group only Miss Levy has an unambiguous joy in her face, perhaps pleased at what she was releasing. There are one or two other smilers, a sly grin, but also a grimness. Crouching in the front row with a sign identifying our school and class, I am doing what is expected—smiling. But athletic Johnny Melnick, Tevya Abramovitch, and two other boys in the front row seem to be looking with suspicion at a future that is outside the frame of the photo, quite distinct from the effervescence of the girls who seem confident about the world and themselves. Was there some secret that we were not privy to, some magic unknown to us that they would use to bring the world to its heels?

The Laurentians

MAGIC DID NOT HAPPEN at Mount Royal School, but when classes let out in June and the family drove thirty miles into the Laurentians it was as unmistakable as a visiting circus. For two months we would become part of Montreal's transplanted population. We'd set off, our car packed with clothes, pots and pans, until finally no room was left except for a narrow space on top of blankets and pillows which my brother and I wedged ourselves into.

We were not alone. By July, the streets of my neighborhood had gone silent, emptied of the shouts of children. Many of them had gone off to summer camps, some operated by charities that charged nominal fees. As late as 1959, the Habonim Camp Krutza in Lac Carré asked no more than $130 for a 4 week stay or $250 for 8 weeks (with $7 for return bus fare, seventy-five cents weekly for laundry, and one dollar per week for insurance). But more often, as in our case, it was not only children, but whole families leaving town, with fathers staying for the weekends and returning to their factories and shops for the workday week.

In the early evening of a summer Friday, a teenager rising to full height on a ferris wheel at Belmont Park would have seen a procession of automobiles, bumper to bumper, approaching the bridge at Cartierville, each impatiently waiting to cross the northern branch of the St. Lawrence—we called it the Back River—to a succession of villages. Those villages had often been named after favorite sons; that is, until the mid-nineteenth century when Ignace Bourget, Montreal's second bishop, sent religious orders to settle the north. From that time on, villages took on the names of saints or martyrs—St. Martin, St. Agathe, St. Faustin, St. Jovite—thereby acquiring the ring of piety that the provincial clergy felt befitted the descendents of New France's pilgrim farmers. Nevertheless, some villages, like Lesage and Mont Rolland, had favorite sons with an identity strong enough to resist induction into this holy army.

Belmont Park roller-coaster.

What the long line of autos passed could only be described as haphazard—a general store close to the road, its owner in a straw hat nodding at the traffic stopped at a light; a two story house with porches upstairs and down, beside an empty lot with stacked cords of wood; and, further from town, fields with shoots of corn that would be harvested in the fall for cattle feed. After a few miles, when Montreal's tallest buildings had disappeared from the rear view mirror, the highway, route 11, continued north on to Val Morin, Val David, and Préfontaine, where many of those autos unloaded their passengers.

In Préfontaine, where we spent one summer, the affluent few stayed in Rosen's Hotel, which sat up on a hill, but most of us rented space below in what looked like a barracks, but was actually a series of attached two- rooms-and-a-kitchen shacks that had been jerry-built for summer migrants. All that separated one unit from another was a wall of pine, no more than a quarter-inch thick with knotholes like those that my brother and I pressed our ears against to eavesdrop on our neighbors' conversations or peered through to view Botero-like matrons stepping out of their undergarments.

The renters' shacks buzzed with children, whom we met outside on a dusty lot that had long ago lost its grass and flimsy plantings to the scuffing of running shoes. Only by the nearby North River were there grasses tall and dense enough to maintain the illusion of a rural

Laurentian landscape. The river there was shallow, almost motionless. Sunning themselves on boulders, mothers buried their toes in the muddy river bottom while we children dumped pails of mud sludge on the narrow edge—hardly a beach-- that separated the grasses from the river. While we waded and splashed one another, two or three older children fished from shore, moving their rods slowly back and forth. Heads turned when the line stiffened and a struggling bass or limpid sucker was flipped onto the shore. Both looked uncomprehending, with lips open but with nothing to impart.

At the top of the hill, life was placid. On the hotel verandah, between sips of tea, well heeled matrons peered through the railing to track any disruptive sound from the shacks below—a mother screaming, a child crying—before resuming their games of rummy or canasta.

The highlight of the week was Friday night, when the renters drifted down the slope to the railway station where the father of the family—if he owned no automobile—would appear for the weekend. From a distance smoke signaled the imminent arrival of the ponderous black engine, immense to the eyes of a child. With one last wheeze the engine came to a stop, fathers stepped out with valises (several tied with rope), the conductor shouted, and, after a shudder, the train chugged around the bend and out of sight.

Trains of my childhood, 1940s.

Seen from the outside, the engine was massive, the puffs of steam from its cheeks a mystery of energy. But inside, I discovered on those rare occasions when I rode the train to our summer cottages, it was more a miracle than a mystery. Looking out the window was no mere passing of time. Like books, the windows became the eyes that enabled me to learn. It was as though I were not so much staring out a window, as following a film strip of disconnected images: the loading dock at the rear of a textile factory, the winding of a river, the grazing cattle, the random barns. Suddenly the choices were enormous. Each of those images was ready to receive me, to absorb me into its story. I did not realize then what writers eventually do realize, that fictions are everywhere, like air. What I did grasp was the ease with which one could break through the enclosures that the physical world imposed and enter the worlds that one's imagination chose. Trains have always had a magic for me; they still do.

Going by Rail

you soon forget the starting
point, heavy columns, porters
you brush by to dimming light,
the slow movement past monuments
you lived close to, abandoned
cars, as twilight tumbles eyes
of suburban windows you rush by,
your own eyes staring through
interruptions of boxwood groves,
the algebra teacher across from you, open
to fractions, your first dinner, a slice
of something whose trip has ended
and some dessert you set aside.

But you remember the prairies—everything
becomes prairie, even waves
of hills succeeding one another, hulks

of mills lengthening in midday sun
along snake dark water, back hoes
forgotten, and hulls of Ford
pickups rusting in backyards,
their red becomes prairie.

You take suburbs by surprise
bisecting duck paths, grazing
the local zoo where long horn sheep
gaze as though remembering
something else moving beyond
their wired country; you pass
the loading dock of a post office,
two loaders heaving a half dozen bags,

lurch by smoking chimneys,
rear wooden porches. Crossings
where locals spar
at the local gym tap
the light bag of your memory
until you become this countryside
where hung out laundry breathes
you, folds you in each gust,
takes you in—unembarrassed—
a stranger with only loose change
and no official papers.

My first trip to the Laurentians and several thereafter was not to
Préfontaine but to the foothills, in farmer Leblanc's fields in Lesage,
by a river where summer renters swam and fished. That was where
I saw for the first time a world entirely different from the brick and
stone structures that I passed from September to June. As soon as I
stepped into the open air, I smelled the farmyard: the cows, chickens
and pigs; the stacked hay; the rich manure that filled the air from
the neighboring barn by the paved highway and carried across
fields into a wood. Here for the first time I was charmed by the
supercilious stare of cows, by the way chickens shed their warmth

The family at farmer Leblanc's in Lesage, Quebec.

along paths that they created. I accepted their mooing and clucking as language to be taken seriously. The openness of the fields, the orchestra of barnyard sounds and nocturnal chat of cicadas spoke to me of endlessness. No teachers, no books, only pastures to gaze at or games to play with other children until we were all covered in darkness. For two months I careened through a world of laughter and shouting with no parental referees. It was as though they had ceased to exist, and I find it ironic now to stare at the only photo I have of those days—not a snapshot of the wonderful chaos of play, but a family photo, taken on the weekend when my father came from hammering out the dents in cars in order to plunge into the North River and store up sun for the coming week. The farm provided its own surprises whenever our play became too predictable. Kick the can was our daily game, a variation on hide and seek, but with the added pleasure of kicking an empty tin can into improbable shapes and improbable places. One day the tin landed in brush where Mr. Leblanc had laid a trap in order to put an end to the nightly assault of skunks on his chickens. Finally one of the traps had snapped shut. Robert, the farmer's son, was young enough to love animals, but not old enough to shy away from a sleek furry creature. As he stooped to pat it, the skunk did what skunks do. Though Robert was bathed repeatedly, for the remainder of the summer none of us would play with him. As for the skunk, the farmer ended its career with one blow of a bough across its head.

Mr. Leblanc had no ducks or geese, but he did keep a couple of pigs, whose tenancy turned out to be brief. Shadowing my idyllic memories of the farm was a late August ritual which brought the farmer's brother and grown nephew from a neighboring town. On that day, the pig selected for the occasion departed from its habit of snuffing around the barn for slops; it fidgeted, tried to move away from the humans approaching. Before long the farmer and his brother had trussed the pig's legs while the other members of the family held the pig on its back. As the Leblanc family hovered like a team of surgeons, it responded with squeals which were as close to a human sound as I have ever heard coming from an animal. That was the last we heard before its throat was slit. Not long after that, perhaps two or three days, our family car was packed again—my brother and I wedged in our places—and pointed toward Clark Street. Somehow it was fitting that the summer ended with that porcine dirge. It was our way of learning that even summer idylls come to an end and that the days of summer finally have their nightfalls and their frosts.

Paperman's Funeral Parlor was barely visible from our rear balcony on Clark Street, but from time to time, I made out its hearses moving slowly along St. Urbain Street past the synagogue to cemeteries on the outskirts of the city, a sonority in the air, the iconography of death, but not death itself. The death of a classmate, Ben Ami Hill in the second grade, brought the event closer. Over the years he has dimmed in memory to an oval face, whose features I cannot make out. He died from tuberculosis at a time when other sufferers were sent to a sanatorium outside St. Agathe for a mountain cure. As far as I was concerned, it was not as though something cataclysmic had happened. He was absent one day, then another. No one answered when his name was called. And then it wasn't. He simply disappeared. But that pig, a distinct grunting presence for every day of two months, squealing to its last moments, brought a whole shudder and curtain closing finality to life as I returned to Mount Royal's classrooms for further instruction.

Back on the Street

THE WORLDS OF MY CHILDHOOD—family, school, neighborhood—rarely intruded on one another. While in school, I never thought about the neighborhood children, nor was school in my thoughts in our packed car bound for the Laurentians in late June. And when we ran in a pack through our street games as school resumed in September, our summer escapes had already faded from memory. They weren't necessary. There was a life entire on the streets. In the fall, in front of Mount Royal School, we played touch football with a stuffed stocking and marveled at how high it would rise when "Meatball," the largest kid on the block, put his foot to it. Immense when measured in any direction, Meatball was an equalizer in any neighborhood scrap, and at the head of a group of stragglers discouraged any aggression when we wandered outside the neighborhood. In winter, we played street hockey, sliding without skates along the packed snow and ice of Clark Street. Hockey sticks were cheap; skates weren't. As soon as school was out at 3:30 we sprinted home for sweaters and hockey sticks. Dribbling a puck, which slid so easily along the packed surface through imaginary goal posts, usually two clumps of ice, we played as darkness fell, the street lamps came on and we heard the cries for supper coming from our front porches.

In retrospect, our shouts resounding through the icy air were the heraldry of neighborhood, such as rarely exists any longer in North America. After World War II ended immigrant factory hands left the heart of the city for detached homes or duplexes with small plots of land in outlying neighborhoods. They called this suburban death "moving up." One family, one set of walls. A family per box. The surrender of community for a few shrubs and flowers that bloomed only briefly before the frost leveled them, leaving empty pavement and a ghostly quiet on the streets. During my years in Montreal we were spared another demographic nightmare, the raising of high-rise slums for the poor, which intensified the number of people living close to one another, lowering the kindling point at which intimacy turns to violence.

In school, I had learned the means by which people reckon and read, some anchor points of time and space in history and geography, a few grammatical elements in French, and some of the pleasures of art and music, though my own attempts at painting looked—still look—pitiful. But it was the neighborhood that completed my education, giving me a texture of daily life, a tapestry of triumph, loyalty, fear, and, one evening, terror.

Halloween was less an occasion for gathering candy treats than an opportunity to play tricks. One Halloween night, we chose to torment a neighbor, a figure with a large, meaty face, thick moustache over a thick upper lip, and a loud voice. By attaching a series of elastic bands to one another, we managed to create a thrumming sound on his window pane. We waited half hidden so that we would not be seen until he roared out of his front door, naked from the waist up, hairy, broad chested, and looking as though he would devour anything that he could lay his hands on. There was enough distance between Mr Schwartzenberg and us to ensure our safety if we didn't linger. We didn't. We ran until we could neither see nor hear him. Even then I could imagine him running in giant steps over mountains and ocean to overtake us, tracking us into the remotest of caves with a thrumming elastic in his hand and a fury in his voice. Since then I have seen monsters represented in literature and film, but never anything so gripping to me as the sight of his ferocious shape.

Such images and memories continue to grip my imagination; they promise more than a treasury of anecdotes to be served up at a dinner party. Only recently have I begun to understand what those images provide, specifically how they highlight the way in which childhood and neighborhood survive in my memory. Nothing has clarified the process more forcefully than a pair of paintings from a catalogue of Edouard Vuillard's work. In the first, the singer, Yvonne Printemps is the focal point. Almost at the centre of the canvas and once again the famous chanteuse of the day, she invites me to listen to her throaty rendering of "Plaisir d'Amour," to notice the flush on her cheek and her well defined hands, so unlike the idealized hands of the other portrait. She is once again under floodlights, and, closing my eyes, I become her audience. But it is in the other painting that I come to know her more deeply than I ever could as a member of an audience. Here, lounging on a sofa, Printemps is presented as one blossom among many. The very atmosphere is redolent of blossoms, the room turning into blossoms, the wallpaper breathing them. She herself is not so much the center of a picture as a summary of it. In these studies, Vuillard is experimenting with ways of seeing, ways of knowing. And in this painting in which the attention to detail is given not to the figure, but to the surroundings of blossoms, it is by these surroundings that we know her.

When we try to define ourselves, to excavate ourselves from lost time, it becomes difficult, almost impossible to know ourselves apart from our surroundings, the prism through which we see the past. In brushing by Mount Royal School, hearing once again the shouts in the schoolyard and that booming voice on Halloween, seeing once again that fish darting in my Aunt Faige's bathtub, sniffing the scent that Robert had carried from his encounter with the skunk, squirming on my wooden seat as darkness descended on that Yom Kippur congregation in October, I am penetrating a clouded gap of sixty years to retrieve an image of myself at age ten, one that is sharper than what I find in my family photo albums.

Montreal remains a pilgrimage point that I move to sometimes with hesitation, more often impetuously, like a lover. To make the asphalt recede more quickly on my northward drive from Boston, I occasionally sing or recite poems. Housman's "Terence, This is stupid stuff," the penultimate poem in *A Shropshire Lad*, can keep me going for ten minutes, devouring ten miles of the journey. Songs revisited over the years, including those we sang at Baron Byng High, take another bite. I tell myself, there are reasons for visiting Montreal—my publisher is there; so are my brother, his children and a long train of family. Even a piddling excuse, a casual acquaintance, for example, curious about Montreal, will draw me to raise the ghosts of the old neighborhood, describing at length the landmarks of my childhood—the red brick kindergarten, stripped of the screams of morning recess with something in its place that is, paradoxically, both obtrusive and non-descript. The cross on its roof discourages me from inquiring whether it is still a school; I walk away from the site feeling like a solider of Islam who has lost more ground to the crusading knights of France. But the faces of houses on Clark seem the same, perhaps a tree missing here, another added there. So does St Lawrence Boulevard. Mrs. Katz's dressmaker supplies disappeared shortly after her shop (submitting to the new language laws) became Boutonnier Katz. So did Sinclair's, and most recently, Labow, along with his cabinetry of powders and salves. Buses replaced trams. Still the street teems with those who walk through the crossfire of dialogue between the shop fronts on one side and those on the other.

My pilgrimage homeward is never as exhausting as the earlier one pilgrims endured climbing up the rue St. Jacques in Paris and trudging through Normandy and Brittany to visit the shrine at Santiago del Compostella in order to pay homage to the finger bones of St. James—all thirty-nine of them, the skeptics quip. How often they must have lingered in tall grass by the roadside, gulping down something purchased earlier, but from time to time settling into the comfort of an inn. One of my settling places in Montreal was a delicatessen called Schwartz, reputed to sell the best smoked meat in the city. Perhaps. I do remember the earlier Schwartz with its floor that slanted, though no one had the temerity to prove it by rolling a glass from one side to the other. The floor is tiled now, the restaurant a favorite of Francophones, and no longer a gathering place for those European Jews who worked in the textile factories.

Still, as I walk along familiar streets, I find my private arborway, where memories have been preserved, where swarms of kids swipe at a puck on the snow packed street, kick a can or bounce a ball off the lumber yard wall.

PART TWO

Slouching Towards Manhood

DURING MY YEARS AT Mount Royal, World War II was being waged. But for children not yet in their teens, the war was like a distant rumble—there, but miles away and unthreatening. Still, it was impossible to be unaware that something serious was happening. Whenever the topic shifted to the war, laughter dropped out of the conversation in the barber shops and at Nathan's or Horn's. At home, when my mother and father fingered the maps of the front in the *Montreal Star*, my brother and I sensed that we were to keep silent. Nor did we laugh at the caricatures of Hitler, Tojo and Mussolini on the editorial page. We knew that they were not like the comic characters in the movies shown on Saturday morning at school. Through the schoolyard fence, we could see the funeral processions leaving Paperman's with flags announcing the death of another Jewish soldier, sailor or flyer.

I tried to imagine them as they might have been, so unlike the shop owners and factory workers on St. Lawrence, who never leapt out of trenches or bivouacked in the mud. Later I realized that these recruits, turning to give photographers a last puckish smile as they boarded their troop ships, were youngsters, some of them no more than a dozen years older than myself. I screwed my eyes to those smiles, looking for a clue to those standards they followed and judged themselves by.

Many years later, the opening take of the film, *The Apprenticeship of Duddy Kravitz*, based on Mordecai Richler's novel, revived that memory of those young recruits. In the darkness of the movie theater, the student cadets marching out of step, their uniforms, loose and baggy, would become part of that procession bound for the sea and from there to the front. I continue to see them—spirited, awkward—as they slip from our reach. In order to recall them, I wrote a few lines and prodded them into the following poem.

Homecoming

Whenever I saw Harry Flatt pumping notes
through his tuba, the clump of them
taking off like a gooney bird
plopping on his gold epaulettes,
and Harry hopping to keep in step
in the homecoming parade,
I knew the sky had opened
for redemption, for all of us,
for the droolers and nose pickers,
even Harry who would crawl up to heaven
on all fours, or get sucked up, his hair
standing like a corn crop.

And the band marked time
(notes slicked down like an old Ford
stuck in second gear, except
they weren't stuck and jolted on)
in whites and reds as red
as fireplugs, until it broke
up at Howard's where sodas
spilled over glass, and everyone
laughed like hussars.

It was forty or forty-one when
the letters came, typed up from the board,
and the whole band signed up,
even Harry Flatt, hair rising
like an expectation
and the war kissed them,
even the sophisticates
from Leopard Hill and Lafayette,

laid them down like children and spread
an eternity of white crosses
like corn seed
in longer and longer rows and the birds

flew north, whole flocks of them,
and never stopped,
not even for crumbs.

If those flocks of birds had paused long enough and conde-
scended to study us, as we often study them, they would have noticed that the inhabitants of Montreal's Jewish district were not
a homogeneous group: some were those young recruits stepping
towards manhood; others looked as though they had come from
the Poland of an earlier century, women with kerchiefs covering
wigs, men in broad brimmed hats, long black coats, striding to the
synagogue with a confidence that each step they took was directed
by Providence. But most Jews did not go so far. They dressed like
anyone else and attended synagogue services only on high holidays.
Otherwise they expressed their Jewishness by reading an occasional Yiddish newspaper—for my father it was the *Keneder Adler* (the
Canadian Eagle), Montreal's Jewish daily, and occasionally the *For-
vertz* (the Forward), a working class paper from New York—and by
seeing that their children consorted with other Jews, and that bar
mitzvahs marshaled their sons into adulthood.

At the age of eleven, in preparation for that ritual, I began my
brief career at the Folks Shule on St. Urbain Street, walking through
its doors only a half hour or so after I left Mount Royal School.
Spending what remained of daylight—in winter there was so little of it—to learn a language that none of my friends on the street
spoke made no sense to me and, worse, interfered with my limited hours of play. So, although the classroom in the Folk Shul was
brighter than Mount Royal's dismal rooms, the students fewer, and
the atmosphere more buoyant, I begrudged my presence there, and
one day in a fit of pique, took a swing at one of the male teachers. I cannot remember why I lashed out. Was it frustration with
the incomprehensible squiggles on the page of a Yiddish text, was
it the songs I didn't understand, or the feeling that I belonged in
some other place? Whatever the reason, I was sent home with a note

Brief stay at the Folks Shule. George (1st row, 2nd from left) reflecting.

which required me to return with my parents. The following day the three of us met with the principal and teacher, who rose from their chairs to greet my parents with warm smiles and extended hands. My parents smiled back sheepishly as if acknowledging some measure of culpability. Both the principal and teacher described my consistent hostility to all that happened within the school, ushering my parents into their account with an indulgent smile. I felt like a spectator, drawn to attention only by the fact that the name they repeated was unmistakably mine. No one looked in my direction, or expected any response from me. If my parents had come to offer pleas for my reinstatement, they were immobilized by what they heard. The consensus was that everyone's best interest would be served if I were removed from the school. I had the decency to pretend that it was a family disgrace and contented myself with an inward celebration at my newly won freedom. I could now join the liberated street hockey players or turn the radio on to *Terry and the Pirates* and *Hop Harrigan*.

My newly won freedom was no more than a reprieve. I was about to turn twelve, and compared with my playmates totally unprepared for my bar mitzvah and the passage into manhood that it marked. My mother was not about to let the year drift by. I rummaged through the assortment of excuses—sore arm, sore leg, sore back—that I had used to avoid school exams, but I found none that would help. And so, after a few months, I surrendered those wonderful free hours and mounted the winding stairs to a second story flat where I would spend late afternoons for the next year. The door was opened by an elderly lady, slight, bent over, with her arms folded across her body as though she were straining to retain body heat, even when the blast furnace of a Montreal summer raised the temperature above 95 degrees. This was the wife of Rabbi Scharb, the instructor my parents hired for five dollars a month to shepherd me to manhood. Once I crossed the threshold, I entered the world of Eastern Europe's shtetls my parents had left. Dominating what must have been a living room before Rabbi Scharb occupied the premises was a long table with benches on either side filled with students, each wearing a skull cap and staring at his text. Rabbi Scharb was shaped like the snowmen we built during the winter, with a round trunk and a round head, joined by an indeterminate neck; his only other snow-like feature was a permanent unshaven stubble of white, made all the whiter by the black suit that he invariably wore. He was a miracle, not only in creating an image of seventeenth century Poland in his Clark Street flat, but in his seclusion from the outside world, like a rotund potted plant in a solarium.

Since his reputation rested on his pupils' ability to read Hebrew, he saw to it that most of them read like speed readers. They never hesitated, skimming across the page like gulls over water, realizing that after each had read twice, Rabbi Scharb would begin to dismiss them, two or three at a time. My movement across the page was more like that of a goony bird, coming to abrupt starts after an ambitious take-off. Anxious not to delay my classmates from being released, I began to read in a state of panic. Before my eyes, the letters tumbled into one another in a drunken melee which I could not untangle, certainly not at a satisfactory speed. I soon collapsed into a stutter, my voice rising and falling, like an automobile lurching when a novice driver releases the clutch too abruptly. Appalled at the prospect of a failure, especially when my brother had been a stellar performer at his bar mitzvah, Rabbi Scharb finally interrupted me one afternoon with some choice gravelly phrases, "Die trombeniak, die bastard voss du bist," (tramp, bastard that you are). In the face of this harangue, the freedom of spirit I had shown at the Folk Shul deserted me. The rabbi was someone I was not about to challenge. Slowly raising my head, I realized that he was now seated opposite me, a lollypop stick in his hand. In order to force me to read more slowly and accurately, he made it clear that I was to intone a syllable as long as he held the stick on that syllable. The minutes moved painfully; everyone around the table fidgeted with impatience as I sounded out the syllables, bohhhhhhhh…rooooch, each one for lengthy seconds, before the lollypop stick moved on to the next syllable. The extra time we spent in class because of my verbal failings generated a quiet hostility among my fellow pupils that simmered but never quite exploded.

Before I left Rabbi Scharb forever I was destined to fall under the shadow of his disapproval a second time. The crisis came shortly before my grand appearance in the synagogue. By this time my performances before Rabbi Scharb were supposed to be dress rehearsals, nothing more. After all, through the intercession of the lollypop stick I was now able to read Hebrew with accuracy. But with just two weeks to go, the rabbi discovered that I had no sense as to what the *trup* signified, those squiggles which indicated how words were to be chanted. His mood shifted from surprise to apoplexy. Too disturbed to instruct me himself, his face flushed beneath the white stubble, he directed one of my benchmates to sing the *trup* signs with me in the privacy of an adjoining room. The Rabbi's reaction convinced me that reading the *trup* would be as daunting as interpreting the language on the Rosetta Stone, but it was no more complicated than a dog learning to fetch a stick, and before the afternoon was out, I was able to leave with the Rabbi's grudging satisfaction, at least to the point where he felt comfortable calling at my parents' home.

He generally visited the bar mitzvah students' parents with some frequency before the event, where he would devour whatever was placed before him in combinations that astonished even my mother, who had witnessed her share of strange behavior. But pickled herring with honey cake was too much, even for her. As for my father, as soon as he heard the door bell, he retreated into the bathroom and emerged only when he heard the door shut behind the departing rabbi. My last memory of Rabbi Scharb is in one of my bar mitzvah photographs, smiling behind a plateful of food. At celebratory meals he could always be found leaning on a table, as reliable as a peasant in a Breughel canvas.

In his autobiography, *The Bread of Time*, the American poet Philip Levine describes an epiphany he experienced while translating a piece by the Spanish writer, Antonio Machado. Confronted by the phrase, "la calle vieja," Levine realizes that its meaning fractures as soon as it is rendered into English as "old street." There is no such thing as an old street in Levine's urban America. One building is replaced by another; a majestic beech is cut down; the haunted house painted into respectability; a corner store leveled for a parking lot, soon to become the branch office of an insurance company. The past evanesces into an eternal present. European writers, on the other hand, inhabit a geography rooted in the past. When they look around them, they see beginnings that anchor them to childhood, whether it is a public square, a parish church, a guildhall, or old streets. American writers seeking such connection flee to Europe as Ezra Pound and T.S. Eliot did.

This burying of the past is happening in my native Montreal as well. The grinding teeth of construction machines have reshaped the downtown so that the once most prominent structure, the Sun Life Building, is now dwarfed by high rise office buildings, apartments, and hotels. In the suburbs construction machines have leveled treed lots and left in their wake rows of detached houses so similar to one another that they seem to have come from a single set of parents. But my old neighborhood and its architectural eccentricities have largely survived along with the shops on St. Lawrence though they now have new names, and the aromas escaping from restaurants identify fresh ethnic groups.

Nevertheless, a major landmark of my childhood, the synagogue in which I celebrated my sudden plop into manhood, has disappeared. For years after it was demolished in 1960, the land on which it stood served as a parking lot, probably because its owner was unsure as to which form of development would bring the greatest return. Fifty years later an apartment building squats on the site.

For years I associated the grandeur of this synagogue chosen for my bar mitzvah with a lengthy and distinguished history. It was considerably larger than the Beth Shloime at the corner of Bagg and Clark Street, which we attended on Rosh Hashanah and Yom Kippur, and seemed originally to have been constructed for Jews more affluent than the garment workers who lived in the surrounding streets and in my immediate neighborhood. On the Sabbath and high holidays the faithful and unfaithful streamed through its twin doors under a large arch and a Star of David. Surrounded by benches at the centre of the synagogue, I stood on the *bimah*, a raised altar, facing a velvet curtain behind which was the Torah scroll that contained my bar mitzvah text. Before long, it was placed in front of me, opened to the passages that had become familiar. Under the starred ceiling of the New Adath Yeshurun Hadrath Kodesh, I sang out my portion of the text, confident that by doing so I was following in the footsteps of generations who had stood there before me. Only later did I realize that I had been deluded; the synagogue, in fact, was no more than thirty years old.

No less disappointing was the discovery that the synagogue had changed its identity as often as a coquette changes her clothes. At its inception in 1917, it was registered as "Hebrew Synagogue"; in

The New Adath Yeshurun Synagogue on St. Urbain near Mount Royal.

the following year as "Adath Yeshurun Synagogue"; five years later, it added "New" to its name. New in what sense? Disgruntled? Unhappy with a change in ritual? Or with the system of purchasing seats for the holidays? Possibly heretical? I am left to create its history.

What is especially strange is that the synagogue seems to have been ambulatory. Before 1926 the Lovell's Directory lists it at 1501 St. Urbain "north of Mount Royal"; in 1926, the same address is identified as "south of Mount Royal." Historians would probably conclude that the directory, erroneous on other occasions, had slipped up here as well. I prefer to see the synagogue as no less restless than some of its neighbors and after a stay of several years on one side of the street, perhaps motivated by the inadequate view, the lack of afternoon sun, or sheer boredom, it simply moved through the darkness to take up its residence on the opposite side. A neighborhood miracle.

I am attached to the day of my bar mitzvah by the thin layer of anticipation I felt that morning in the synagogue. Though my family was seated close by, even my Uncle Meyer, who had come from New York, I did not need them to put me at ease. I had by this time formed a companionship with those syllables and strange signs that I could read and sing, though still without understanding as much as a single word. The event—series of events, since there was a snack at the synagogue, a reception at home, and a banquet at Moishe's Steak House—transformed me for weeks as I saw myself not walking but strutting into manhood.

In the articles of the neighborhood, I had completed the journey into manhood. But it was a journey laced with humor, self-indulgence, absurdity, which ended with gifts of cash stuffed into my wallet and fountain pens into my chest of drawers. I had not yet become aware of the distance between my newly acquired manhood and those recruits walking the plank towards Juno beach and the battlefields of France and Germany.

Baron Byng High School

In truth, my emergence from childhood into adolescence did not come from anything so sudden as a bar mitzvah. Or even from the daily ritual that followed, a winding of leather straps around the forehead and left arm to hold in place phylacteries, small boxes with copies of ancient Hebrew law, a reminder of the obligation to keep faith. For the first two or three days, drawn by the novelty of the experience, I rose dutifully as dawn was breaking, wound the straps so that the phylacteries were firmly set, and recited words whose meanings even today remain a mystery. By the end of the week, the phylacteries had been moved to the back of a drawer.

My walk to Baron Byng High at age twelve had introduced me to another world: crossing Rachel Street was like crossing the Jordan into a new geography with new longitudes and latitudes, much to be discovered. My daydreaming leapt to those explorers introduced in elementary school, the bearded coureurs de bois, Radisson and Groseilliers, portaging through woods and down rapids into the Canadian interior. My old neighborhood leaned against a darkness I had rarely penetrated as a child, but now I imagined exploring like those figures I had read about, curious about nearby streets as well as remote areas in the history, geography and literature books I stumbled on. Their novelty gripped me more than the daily winding of straps which never, though meant to, conjured a spiritual helmsman steering the planets, and while leaving indentations on my arm and forehead, left little in my imagination.

The name Baron Byng itself, which sounded grand, even aristocratic, plunked my fantasies well before my first class. After all, my older cousins, Aunt Faige's two sons, were graduates, and by the time I arrived, my brother had been there for two years. I knew that Baron Byng (named after Julian Byng, who had led the Canadian forces at Vimy Ridge in 1917) had been the path for lawyers, doctors, engineers, pillars of the community, and, I was to discover later, the school ground for some of Canada's eminent writers, among them Irving Layton and Mordecai Richler. (Only later did I squirm when I came across a reference in Voltaire's *Candide* to an Admiral Byng of the Royal Navy, Julian Byng's ancestor, who had been publicly executed for cowardice during the Napoleonic wars.)

Nothing at the school was taken casually. It was known not just for certain celebrated alumni, but for the achievement of its students who habitually placed among the highest in the provincial exams that we took upon leaving high school. The reach for excellence extended beyond the academic. The school choir, with half of the student body participating, had its concerts aired on the radio. And although hockey and football were sports the school could not afford, the trophy cases beside the principal's office bulged with statues and cups won in basketball, soccer, and water polo. We had not yet learned the implications of the word, "renaissance," but there was a spirit of something in the school akin to the ideals that Thomas Arnold cultivated at Rugby.

Mount Royal Elementary School, with its dreary interior, had been like a holding station; Baron Byng, with a light that permeated its wide corridors, was more inviting, an Athens that promised to open worlds to all the boys and girls in the neighborhood. What we soon discovered was that we would be separated from the girls for the next four years. In the morning the boys entered from narrow, seedy Clark Street, the girls from wider, more upscale St. Urbain. During lunch and recess, the girls congregated at Moe's, sipping milkshakes while the boys wedged into Mr. Fried's Clark Street hamburger joint, shrieking among the spatterings of grease. Inside, we discovered that boys and girls were taught in different parts of the school, and in the senior grades took different subjects. For example, the girls studied biology, but were shut out from classes in physics and chemistry. Perhaps those who felt that girls lacked the capacity for those disciplines had also concluded that boys could not be trusted with a knowledge of the human body.

On a recent visit to Montreal to attend my high school reunion, I found myself once again approaching Baron Byng High, struggling to recover what I experienced when I first entered at age twelve: the narrow schoolyard, the concrete basement with ping pong tables that brought me to school a whole half hour early, even on the coldest days of January; the hands reaching for hamburgers at Mr. Fried's; the school uniforms—girls in dark tunics and white blouses; and the patriotic songs, "The Maple Leaf Forever" and "The British Grenadiers" that we sang with gusto. But walk as I might along the corridors, looking for plaques on the wall or ping pong tables in the basement, I saw myself as an alien. The space within the walls had been reconfigured for the current occupants, the Sun Youth Organization. And the ghosts of the previous occupants did not respond to my humming of the school song. If they had, I imagine they would have been their old selves—graceless, boisterous—more like gooney birds than gulls, plopping into the water after awkward starts. Yet aloft long enough and with enough zest to make an imprint and like Kilroy, a poster figure in those times, declare, "I was here." Present and truculent.

Baron Byng High School on St. Urbain.

Schools that have not been flattened by the wrecking ball of urban renewal acquire a history. Ours was built around our teachers—we referred to them as masters. Those who approached us with a mastery of their subjects we mythologized, not only listening intently to them, but copying into our lined notebooks each nuance of their arguments and their exact phrases. Among those teachers was Mr. Zweig, who taught math in the early high school grades. Though to the casual eye he would have been undistinguishable in any crowd, he taught to attentive classes, scribbled x's and y's on the blackboard, and finally turned to face us with a half smile under his bristling moustache as equations balanced like a lid closing neatly on a box, with only a soft puff of sound. For me, Mr. Zweig was an overgrown scout leader who guided me through a confusion of brambles into open fields of clarity. It mattered too that Mr. Zweig was Jewish. The only other Jewish teacher in the school was Miss Kadish, the drama teacher. Plump and dimpled, she approached the classroom with a sack of anecdotes that might have been assembled from the programs of ethnic humor on evening radio. She saw herself as a Jewish comedienne, the Molly Picon of Baron Byng. But to us she was more like the maiden aunt, who desperately wanted our laughter and our love, and whose gaucheries we indulged because of age or infirmity. There was no point in humiliating her.

But to those teachers who postured as figures of authority in order to conceal their ineptitude, we were merciless, planning class disruptions with the care of thieves casing a bank. For our inept physics teacher with diminished hearing, we cultivated the skill of speaking without moving our lips. For our chemistry teacher, who blustered "nothing goes over my head but the clouds," we staged a fake stabbing of one student by another with an effusion of watery ketchup to simulate blood. When the principal arrived to restore order, he found each student seated, hands folded, and waiting for instructions. It never occurred to us that our behavior was thuggish, cruel. For us, there was an unwritten pact: teachers had to show mastery in the classroom. If they didn't, we gave ourselves free rein.

Graduating class, Baron Byng, 1951.

Mr. Fleming, my home room teacher in the eighth grade, was barely competent and therefore neither mythologized nor tormented. Like other teachers who made little difference in our lives, he was simply tolerated. He taught us English, which he spoke passably, and French, which was as foreign to him as it was to us, though like us, he had grown up in a predominantly French speaking province. We suffered his bonhomie laughter, looked forward to his absence, and were lightly amused by the erection in his trousers, as he explained points of grammar, lingering on subordinate clauses and compound-complex sentences. And at those moments when we laughed *with* him rather than *at* him, we felt a residual sense of self-betrayal, as though we had given of ourselves too lightly; to snicker was easier.

We never snickered at Miss Zucker. Scarcely five feet tall, she filled the classroom as she addressed the struggles between parliament and the Stuart monarchs. Though James and Charles were no closer to us than a blue-footed booby, they became progressively real and important as we listened to Miss Zucker's indictment of whimsical and capricious monarchy. It was as though John Locke or Thomas Jefferson were standing by the blackboard, piecing together the foundations of human rights. No eyes drifted towards the window or consulted the hands of the clock. Miss Zucker had given history an identity other than lists of dates, battles, and explorations. We were hers to shape.

She may have been unaware of other elements cooperating with her to focus our wondering and wandering eyes on her seventeenth century events, and by extension, on our own century. Radical newspapers had begun to appear on the counter at Nathan's, in their pages a barrage of arguments for the underdog—blacks in the United States, asbestos workers in Quebec. We transferred their grievances to those victimized by the blundering Stuarts. The inept analogy did not trouble us; we were not aiming at logical precision. Conscripted by the rebelliousness in the air, we absorbed the passion of our Russophilic neighbors, read the petitions circulated by those working for our communist MP, Fred Rose, scorned Adrien Arcand's fascist thugs, and allowed Miss Zucker's words to raise our political eyebrows. At least that. And often, more than that. She drew a world in which events were not merely accidents, but the result of identifiable forces and individuals struggling—like us—for power. I have never read anything of the past, from Thucydides' *Peloponnesian Wars* to McCullough's biography of John Adams without the perspectives that came from her stirring voice. Not a one of my other classes, helpful in their own way, had the high seriousness of Miss Zucker's class.

And yet, in retrospect, there was one light moment, disregarded at the time, that stands for me as a counterpoint. The only non-Jew in our class was Harry Pinder, slender and shy. How he came to our class was a mystery because I had never seen a black family in our neighborhood. Everyone liked Pinder; we had not been taught to exclude those who intruded into our ghetto classrooms. And

Harry, though shy, was always friendly. In the entire year that I knew him—he disappeared after my first year—I'd never seen him without a smile.

One day when Miss Zucker was defending parliament's opposition to Charles, she scanned the classroom to see what effect her arguments were producing. Her eye fell on Pinder's broad smile. Impulsively, she trumpeted his name which resounded off the walls and ceiling as though there were no other sound in the universe but a swelling "Pinder." Pinder maintained his smile. We waited to hear the rest of the argument. Looking back now, I see Pinder, that mysterious presence, with a background as shaded as an epic hero's, raising by his silence another viewpoint. His response to all of her earnestness, to her passion for connecting the dots of history so that we could prepare ourselves to make a better world, was an eloquent smile of futility. It clearly was absurd to him, all of it. The debacle of the Stuarts was too immured in the past to be taken seriously; as for the contemporaneous events taking place in a Europe that was unraveling, they were too massive, too incomprehensible to meddle with. He had come to his own understanding, which permitted him to smile at whatever was looming overhead.

Miss Zucker disappeared after that year. Rumors circulated that she had been either a member of the communist party or, at least, a sympathizer. Although our district had been represented by a communist, the hiring of communist history teachers was another matter. And so Miss Zucker's voice no longer boomed through our classroom. But her habit of poking at the homilies of Montreal's Anglo newspapers, the *Herald, Star,* and *Gazette,* stayed with us.

The overt mission of Baron Byng High was to prepare its students to excel in their final examinations in order for them to migrate in droves to McGill University. The unstated mission was to bring these immigrant children to an admiration of British imperial culture, which, in our teachers' eyes, was humanity's greatest achievement. With the exception of Miss Zucker's class, the glories of the empire and the virtues of capitalism were the ideological bunting in the history that we studied. "I'll tell you what capitalism's given you," raged Mr.McPherson to a class of skeptical students. "It's given you your radios and television sets" (which struck me as an odd thing to say since no one I knew owned a tv). When radical petitions were circulated among the students, the principal, Mr. Patterson, a kindly man, urged in soft but decisive tones that we ignore them. Instead, we ignored him.

Our reaction must have been puzzling to teachers who expected us to become loyal sons of the Empire and to embrace the culture that had given us a globe largely painted in British pink from Piccadilly Circus to Bombay. Their agenda was unambiguous: we were budding citizens, waiting for the next set of shaping hands. Our report cards periodically informed our parents that we were assimilating enough to move towards the professions, and that in addition to arithmetic functions and polysyllabic words, we understood the exalted station of the British Empire in the world.

For all our flirtation with radicalism, however, we were smitten, cowed by much of what we saw in British culture, the very language of As You Like It, read in the ninth grade, with its power and grace, its distance and proximity. Or teachers like Mr. Dunn, Shakespeare's emissary, in our last two grades. Plucking a handkerchief from his jacket sleeve with thumb and index finger, he could with a word lower an obstreperous student to the obsequious level of a dachshund. His manner, which smacked of Oscar Wilde, was something we had not yet experienced, and while making us aware of the power of language, made us also see ourselves as coarse, unlettered, and sub-Colonial, party crashers at a dance whose steps we had not begun to master. A showing of David Lean's production of Great Expectations had the same effect of placing us outside a world where high drama took place. Magwitch emerging from the moors, the forbidding room in which Miss Havisham holds court, Pip's passage into snobbery, fictions witnessed in the darkness of the Kent Theater reminded us that we were not to experience such drama in our houses, suffused with the odors of chicken soup and chopped liver. Plum pudding and the pomposity of Pumblechook, all part of a foreign world, a form of grace fully available to our Christian brethren in Westmount, was rationed out to us in dollops through films or the offerings of our teachers. Nevertheless, the door was open. That distant world had issued an invitation. If we worked hard, played hard, we too could shed the last of our immigrant traces and take our place with other colonials in the expansiveness of the empire.

Heroes

MEANWHILE, SEVERAL classmates and I established our empire at the Neighbourhood House, where in 1948 we formed the Buzz Beurling Memorial Club. It was not the first such institution to serve the Jewish community. As far back as 1910 the majority of those served at the University Settlement House at 159 Dorchester Street West, were Jews who lived south of Sherbrooke Street; by the mid-twenties, that community had shifted to the area north of Sherbrooke, a neighborhood that offered youth no recreation other than street play. A letter sent in 1926 by the Juvenile Aid Department to its board at the Federation of Jewish Philanthropies reflects the concern of parents who felt that the absence of a local Settlement House would result in their children drifting to swaggering, swearing, and scrapping in bowling alleys, delicatessens—one might add, pool rooms—then to juvenile court and, eventually, to Boys' Farm, a correctional facility for juveniles in Shawbridge, thirty miles north of Montreal. Three years later, in response to this concern, a Neighborhood House was established on Laval Street between Napoleon and Duluth, where it remained until the mid-forties.

By the time I arrived at Baron Byng High in 1947, a new Neighborhood House had been built half a block from school, still providing activities designed to keep children off the streets. Not that we had to be dragged to participate. We relished the prospect of playing basketball on the newly varnished gym floor, had somewhat less interest in the arts and crafts program, though some of us devoted time to painting on sheets of thick paper. What most attracted me and my friends were those newly minted rooms that we could occupy if we organized. Clubs had become a fashion, and having seen other students strutting around Baron Byng High with club jackets, we came to consider having a club of our own as a mark of distinction.

Some clubs chose names that suggested vigor or camaraderie, such as the Rockets and Amigos. We chose Buzz Beurling as our

JUVENILE AID DEPARTMENT

A CONSTITUENT SOCIETY OF THE FEDERATION OF JEWISH PHILANTHROPIES

MISS MARY VINEBERG,
CHAIRMAN BIG SISTER COM.

832 ST. URBAIN STREET

PLATEAU 3513

MONTREAL,   **May 28, 1926.**

The Executive Committee,
Federation of Jewish Philanthropies,
2040 Bleury St.,
Montreal.

Dear Sirs;

       The Juvenile Aid Society desires to place briefly
before your Board details of certain conditions existing in a con-
gested district in Montreal, inhabited principally by Jewish people,
which conditions must receive our earliest attention if we are to
prevent a serious increase in delinquency among the Jewish children
there. At the same time this Society wishes to place before you the
method it proposes to adopt, to deal with the situation, and which it
hopes will meet with your approval and support.

       In former years a large proportion of the Jewish
people lived in the district of the University Settlement. The
registered attendance of Jewish children at that Settlement ranged
from 75% to 90% of the total attendance.

       In recent years however, the Jewish population has
moved northward. That section of the city between Sherbrooke St.
and Mount Royal Ave., and St. Urbain and St. Denis Sts., has now
become a very densely populated Jewish district. This district is too
far away for its children to be directed and benefitted by the work
of the University Settlement.

       It is important to note that there are five public
schools in this district, with an enrollment of about 7500 children,
of whom about 75% are Jewish. There is no supervised recreational
centre in this district where children may be absorbed after school
hours and during the school vacation periods, into groups for play,
health instruction, and general development of and respect for good
citizenship.

       The only available place for recreation is Fletcher's
Field at the extreme west end of this district. It is only taken
advantage of by a small number of children in this district, who know
how to avail themselves of this playground and who have the necessary
athletic equipment to enjoy it. The Ys cater to an older group of
boys and girls and have little room for the younger public school
children.

A letter from the Juvenile Aid Department to its Board reflecting
the concern of parents, 1926.

JUVENILE AID DEPARTMENT

A CONSTITUENT SOCIETY OF THE FEDERATION OF JEWISH PHILANTHROPIES

632 ST. URBAIN STREET   PLATEAU 2213

MISS MARY VINEBERG
CHAIRMAN AND SUPER COM

MONTREAL,

- 2 -

The majority of the Jewish children appearing before the Juvenile Court come from this district. This is due mainly to the lack of proper direction of energy.

We have found the delicatessen stores of the Main Street and bowling alleys in the neighborhood, the most popular rendez-vous for adolescent boys and girls. These places stimulate gambling, late hours, and increased demand for spending money etc. Reprimand without the alternative of a substitute more elevating and constructive, only tends to aggravate an already well nourished resentment between "old school parents" and Canadian born children. We would like to organize a settlement house in this neighborhood. We feel that a Settlement is an object lesson in ways and means of living to a community that has need of such education to promote general good standards of citizenship.

We would like very much to embark on this new development of our work as an experimental venture. When the Juvenile Aid Department undertook to look after Jewish children appearing before the Juvenile Court, there was a Jewish population of twenty-seven boys at the Boys' Farm at Shawbridge. For the year 1925 there was an average Jewish population of 9.5 boys, largely because employment, school adjustment, medical attention, education of parents was substituted for punishment. Similarly we hope to prevent the number of arrests by building an attractive program for recreation, which will not only take care of physical energy of the children in the neighborhood, but will at the same time have a real value for character building.

It is pleasant to think of the economic saving effected but how much more gratifying to find that children can be adjusted without resorting to such drastic methods as Courts and reformatories.

The cost for the first year would be approximately as follows:

Salary of Worker	$1200.00	
" " Stenographer	600.00	
Rent	360.00	
Light, Heat, Phone etc.	600.00	
Equipment	740.00	$3500.00

While we have given this matter considerable thought, do not consider these figures in any way final. We merely give them to locate an approximate expenditure.

"We have found the delicatessen stores of the Main Street and bowling alleys in the neighborhood, the most popular rendez-vous for adolescent boys and girls."

inspirational spirit not only because he was a local war hero, who had shot down over thirty planes in World War II, but because he perished while flying from Rome to offer his services to the newly created State of Israel. And so, as a martyr for Israel, he became a hero for us. With air ace Beurling as our spiritual founder and a Neighborhood House staffer as club advisor, we imitated our elders who held meetings, established policies, although our venues were not quite so vast and our decisions limited to the colors of our club cardigan or, indeed, whether a jacket would be preferable to a cardigan. We did find time to organize some events—basketball games, occasional bowling, a discussion of discrimination against Jews and Blacks, an evening with the parents of Buzz Beurling, and a social with a girls club that we invited where I had my first (and last) puff of a cigarette. (Early on, the shrewd among us had

Hon. Joseph R. Nuss in the cardigan of the Buzz Beurling Memorial Club.

pointed out that forming a club would be a good way to meet girls who, during school hours, were segregated in another part of our school, tucked away from us like initiates in a Carmelite order.) But most of our attention was given to form and decorum. After two years of pecking at parliamentary rules, our weekly meetings became as frayed as our maroon and gray club cardigans. The surviving minutes of these meetings held more than fifty years ago mainly record members being sent from the room, usually for talking. One reference has me dispatched to the corridor for swearing. What, I wonder, did I pull out of my limited storehouse of profanity to be paraded for inspection before Buzz Beurling's ghost?

In retrospect, though, it seems odd that we chose Buzz Beurling to be our guiding light, someone whose experience was so remote from ours, whose career took place twenty thousand feet above the sidewalks over which we slogged our way to school. We plucked a hero out of space as though we could find none in our day-to-day life, as though our own landscape was too frozen, too forbidding for any hero to hang around waiting to be identified.

And yet those heroes were there. As we moved through high school, the ones we acknowledged most readily were athletes, though after the hockey season, there was little on the sports front to stir the local population, except for 1946, the year that Jackie Robinson played second base for the Montreal Royals. But, generally, the trip to Delorimier Stadium, the Royals ball park, was no more exciting than a casual Sunday outing. Francophones had limited interest in a team that, with the exceptions of Roland Gladu and Jean Pierre Roy, had no French Canadians. Even for Anglophones, the Montreal Royals were merely a farm team that shone, if at all, in the reflected light of their parent club, the Brooklyn Dodgers. Still, for less than a dollar admission, we could watch Robinson, Duke Snider, John Roseboro, George Shuba, and a young Johnny Podres completing their apprenticeship. We were early observers of their talent as they ascended to a pantheon that we would never visit, their distance from us confirmed by the static-filled rendition of a Dodger's night game on the radio.

In the years immediately following World War II professional football attracted no more interest than baseball. Because a limit was imposed on the number of Americans which any team could sign, most players were Canadian, Anglo-Canadian, which did little to stimulate the interest of Montreal's majority population in the local team, the Montreal Alouettes. But in those months before the streets were buried in winter, it did stir the interest of many of us at Baron Byng, possibly because our school had no football team. From September to November we could witness the ferocity unleashed by the blowing of a whistle and the calling out of numbers. What we saw on the football field took on the character of great battles we had read about—Zama, Culloden Moor, Stalingrad—supplemented by grunts and thuds that sounded out a human earthquake. During those early years, the players who stood out were the "American imports," as they were called, as though they were a special brand of whiskey or automobile. They *were* special, especially those on the defensive line who lunged with the ferocity of Bengal tigers. One afternoon the Montreal Alouettes' quarterback, import George Ratterman, was calling out numbers to his teammates facing the crouched defensive line of the Hamilton Tiger Cats with two import defensive ends, Joe Shinn and Vince Mazza. They moved as soon as the ball moved and before a second had elapsed, they made Ratterman simply disappear. From that time on, Ratterman, for whom great success had been predicted, slipped into obscurity, and, finally, somewhere below the Canadian border. Nothing was more fierce than those import defensive linemen; even import quarterbacks with stellar reputations crumpled before them. When Frankie Albert, who had come to Canada for a year to play quarterback for the Calgary Stampeders, was asked what he thought about Canadian football, he remarked that he hadn't seen much of it since he had spent most of his time either on his back or running for his life.

But baseball, football, and other sports were little more than a hiatus between hockey seasons. And the athletes we prized most were hockey players, especially those who played for the Montreal

Canadians Hockey Club in the Montreal Forum. Tickets to those games we soon learned were a rare possession, often passed on from one generation to the next, and so I became one of the millions of Canadians who resigned themselves to the only alternative, turning their radios on to the Saturday night broadcasts.

Miss Bonhomme, who gave my brother piano lessons and helped my mother sew dresses, stayed overnight with us on those Saturdays while my parents went out with friends. For Miss Bonhomme's sake, I truly hope there is a heaven because she earned it. As soon as my parents were out of sight, we shot through the front door and, with nothing on but briefs, jumped up and down in deep banks of snow. Since all the windows on the street were frosted over, our entertainment was exclusively for Miss Bonhomme who, lost for words, would stand in the doorway and proclaim to the emptiness of the street, "God save the King and the Queen."

Afterwards, we'd pepper her with the most bizarre questions we could frame, such as how the corner grocer farted, or the pope, or the prime minister of France. In response, Miss Bonhomme would produce a variety of sounds that amused us by their virtuosity. All of this was a prelude to the hockey game itself between the Canadians and one of the other five National Hockey League teams. The broadcast picked up the action at nine sharp, after the end of the first period. For me, those broadcasts propelled through electrical wires were a lifeline that joined together the thin population of Canada from Vancouver to Halifax. A hundred miles to the north of that corridor lay darkness, woodland, uncertainty, and no Montreal Canadians hockey broadcast.

As dynasties go, the Canadians hockey team was far more significant to me than the Romanovs, the Hapsburgs, or the Hohenzollerns. Their Saturday night games unfolded like ritual, and, like ritual, were predictable. No one tuning in to those broadcasts expected anything but a Canadians' victory. The only mystery was the final score. When the Forum lights dimmed and the Canadians, led by goalkeeper big Bill Durnan, skated onto the ice, leaning forward and moving in swift circles around the north end of the arena, we knew that we were participating in a religious ceremony where grace was given, redeeming all of us. The certainty of their triumphs was so strong that any interruption in their string of championships was regarded as major floods or landslides are in other countries, and, of course, required a human sacrifice, usually the coach, who learned that in Quebec anything less than a Stanley Cup was a capital offense.

The cheering in the Forum, loud and sustained, convinced us all that we were adherents of the true faith. And I expect that there was a resounding echo in living rooms across Canada, except in Ontario, where the unconverted persisted in cheering on the hated Toronto Maple Leafs. The only non-believer I personally knew was a fellow member of the Buzz Beurling Memorial Club who declared his loyalty to the New York Rangers, one of two teams renowned for its consistent failure to qualify for the Stanley Cup playoffs. It may have been the splendor of Madison Square Garden or the elegant play of Edgar Laprade and Buddy O'Connor (who had been traded from Montreal) that fed his heresy, but he persisted. He was a reincarnation of Harry Pinder, rejecting our iconography, whatever the consequences.

Between periods, eager to find a Jewish player, we would study each name on the Canadians' roster. Maurice "Rocket" Richard? No, there was no way that the French "Maurice" could be construed as a Jewish "Morris." Elmer Lach played beside the Rocket, but there was no Elmer among my Jewish classmates. Kenny Mosdell, though a lesser figure, we would gladly have claimed; "Kenny," though less typical than Hymie or Jack or Joe, had affixed itself to a classmate, and I had a cousin whose last name was similar, off by just one consonant. In baseball, we did have Kermit Kitman, a center fielder who never once hit the ball off the right-field wall at Delorimier Stadium although it was only 293 feet away. So we had to make do with Hank Greenberg who played left field for the Detroit Tigers championship team in 1945. Though not a Montrealer, he was clearly one of us.

Looking back, I puzzle at this compulsion to extract a Jewish constellation from the sports world. After all, as our elders often pointed out to us, Jews had made a mark in music, in philosophy, in the sciences, and in letters, providing the assurance that we had been given some share of the world's wisdom and talent. Yet our hunger for Jewish sports heroes persisted. Perhaps the winters were so long, the dreariness so endless that the only fantasy left to us had streaks of Jewish adolescents skating on frozen ponds, cradling a puck on the blades of their sticks until a happy few skated into the Forum in the uniform of the Montreal Canadians.

Maurice Richard.

So much of our adolescence seems to be a running across fields, striving to outrun the sun itself in the chase after icons. No matter how much rationality is drummed into school curricula—the cold determination of sums, the certainty of geographical borders and historical dates, we cling to the image of a puck driven into a net, a football descending to reaching hands. Of all the icons that passed through my childhood, none was more imposing than Maurice Richard. His death produced not only a mourning across the country, but a suspension of legislative activity in our capital, Quebec City, as mourners followed his casket from Notre Dame

Church on Montreal's Place d'Armes to the Cimetière Notre Dame des Neiges. In a way he had died once before, when he announced in 1958 that he would not rejoin the club. Shortly before that, he was interviewed near the Canadians' bench in the Forum. Staring across the unlit ice, he mused on what was to follow once he gave up careening down the right side of the ice against all obstacles. "I'm afraid" he said. "I've never known anything but hockey. I don't know what I'm going to do." At that moment, Richard, who had become more symbolic than real, suddenly returned to us. The incandescence of heroism, the triumphal coherence of the heroic narrative, for Richard, for all heroes, slips away all too easily under the scourge of daylight, and I found myself once again locked into a routine of prescriptive grammar and the disconnecting sections of intermediate algebra.

Windows of Adolescence

OUR ESCAPE HATCHES from the proprieties of adolescence were never as bizarre as Gargantua's climb to the tower of Notre Dame cathedral, from where he urinates on the bystanders below, but at Baron Byng High, we did have our modest ways of cutting loose, inherited from a generation of students who had come before us. One was our exodus from the school's precincts to the Rachel Billiard Hall, a mere block away on St. Lawrence. While our tenth grade history master, Mr. McPherson, chalked in all the blackboards with justifications of British imperial policy, most of us slipped out of the class, two or three at a time, taking giant steps across the hall into the bathroom. Then, as soon as we were convinced that the halls were empty, we bounded down the stairs, through a door, down a lane, and turned sharply onto St. Lawrence Boulevard. The pool room lay ahead. Leaving a street bedazzled by late afternoon sunshine, we squinted as we entered; in front of us, seven tables, each globed by a circle of overhead light. It was our Friday afternoon oasis where the recital of nineteenth century British conquests gave way to the click of colored balls. Since we spent much time there we developed some skill, though remaining painfully aware of how far short of perfection we fell. Even the two or three players most admired in the school were creatures of a fallen world, who could be counted on to miss the shots that mattered most.

One day, as afternoon had drifted into evening, too early to go home for dinner, too late to do anything else, the door opened and through it stepped someone we'd never seen before. He was not a fellow student, nor was he one of the local characters who had made the pool room a home away from home, pointlessly practicing shots whenever the owner permitted. The stranger hung up his raincoat and walked to an empty table at the rear, opening a case that held a polished pool cue. We had never seen anything like this before—a personal cue, all his own. After setting up the balls he began to play, never pausing between shots, simply strolling to where he knew the ball, after bouncing off one or two, even three, cushions, would come to rest. And when it did, he was already there, waiting to shoot again. With the table cleared, he put his raincoat back on and left. There was no need to say anything, to applaud. Leo Levitt had come down from the planets to show us what perfection was.

Mr. McPherson was also a wizard of sorts. Once, standing on his hands on a chair, he propelled his body into a somersault as though his arms were the supporting members of a machine and his curled trunk a wheel that spun freely. He could also throw three pennies in the air and catch them in quick succession as they fell, persuading us as gullibility set in on late afternoons that he had made his own private arrangements with gravity. We marveled, but only until he slipped back into his role as missionary for the British Empire. In a neighborhood that was Russophilic and the political seat of communist Fred Rose, Mr. McPherson's blackboard sermons on the glories of the British Empire prompted only a few to transcribe his words. The rest of us drifted not only to the Rachel Street Pool Room but also to the Hollywood Theater, a block away, that showed two movies, a cartoon, a travelogue, and the Movietone news heralded by a crowing rooster. What a splendor to leave the harsh sunshine of St. Lawrence Boulevard for the darkness of anonymity where we dropped out of the period between Canning and Gladstone and into the world of Hollywood. I no longer remember specific movies we saw there, only the soothing darkness, the lulling voices on the screen. More memorable were the outings when history class siphoned us all the way to vaudeville at the GayetyTheatre on St. Catherine Street. It was pure pageantry—comics, jugglers, dancers, but best of all, Peaches and Lili St. Cyr, wearing whatever gave them accents that we yearned for, their breasts thrown out as flares to reaching eyes. What did I know of their other lives, unacknowledged to us? Did Peaches doff that cascade of hair and reach for a needle to mainline when she slumped into the privacy of her dressing room? Did Lili, exotica of French

Canada, find an Anglo name like Willis Marie Van Schaack, with an address in Minneapolis, Minnesota when she plucked her driver's license from her purse? Or were they simply versions of housewifery and motherhood? All questions we never asked. Why should we? On those Friday afternoons, between juggling and dinner, they were my all in all—a summary of my cinders of sexual memory—Miss Kastner with opulent breasts whose smile took winter out of the snow, and even the sting of the ruler from our flesh; a twelve-year-old girl who lived on Drolet Street, seen once in the summer with hair the color of which haunts me as color itself fades; the women, purposefully walking down the stairs from a flat on Clark Street where male strangers drifted in and out at unusual times of the day…were they going to the cobbler? or to mail a letter? Did it matter? It had been a while since my body had begun to range out of my rectangular block. My imagination, driven by a fever in the blood, stoked by curiosity, now began to follow.

But as much as we at Baron Byng High and the Buzz Beurling Memorial Club sought opportunities to meet with girls—conversations inevitably came around to them—formal dates were often awkward. It was as though some advisory voice from an unseen world was whispering instructions as to how we should behave. But the instructions differed from one minute to the next. On the one hand we were advised to be gentle and express the tenderness we heard in the crooning lyrics of "Golden Earings" and "The Anniversary Waltz." On the other we were urged to see seduction as an initiation into manhood and woman as a trophy, an achievement that the socially glib would brag about during school recess. There was nothing in this crossfire of messages to reduce the shyness and uncertainty we felt about courtship in general. Added to these contradictory scripts was the weight of conventions that seemed arbitrary and yet as venerable as the rites of courtly love in the Middle Ages. Walking home from a movie with a girl, I recalled a point of street etiquette which required the male to walk on the curb side of the sidewalk. And yet, when we crossed the street, it seemed that our geographies reversed, like a boat spinning around in the wind despite my best efforts to right it. Suddenly I was on the inside, with no graceful way of switching positions. The palm of my hand became watery, the fingers that held her fingers damp. She must have suspected my discomfort, but neither of us acknowledged it, making desultory conversation though my attention was entirely on strategies to move unobtrusively to the curbside.

Such moments remain, stubbornly; they refuse to surrender their place to more flattering memories, but co-exist with them, side by side, part of a past we read in glimpses much the way we read a landscape through the window of a moving train. In such situations most of what we see escapes us; only a few sights remain, a few moments. Some are elevating, others repulsive: the expanse of a cornfield in a flame of sunlight as well as the sludge dumped from the rear of a factory into a canal. Memory makes a place for glimpses of all kinds, even hands moist with anxiety.

Heavy traffic on St. Lawrence Boulevard, early 1950s.
Courtesy of André Vigneau, Societé de transport de Montréal.

MOUNT ROYAL AND THE GRADE schoolers that I passed on my way to Baron Byng High had by now become an assemblage of miniatures chasing one another in games of tag. If I noticed them, it was not as individuals but, like starlings and sparrows, as members of a flock. My life had shifted, though less obtrusively than those jolting gears in the automobiles that my father drove during the war.

I did not realize at the time that his life had also changed. Drawing on his savings, he had formed a partnership in 1945 with another

Mrs. J. Ellenbogan

DRESSMAKER

4175 Clarke Street   Montreal

HARBOUR 6414   RES. BELAIR 3584

Royal Auto Body & Radiator Co.

Body, Fender & Radiator Repairs
Painting & Upholstering

REP. BY
   M. ELLENBOGEN   1020 LAGAUCHETIERE ST. W.

immigrant tinsmith who shared his passion for hammering metal, and together they had hung out a sign, "Royal Auto Body & Radiator Co. Ltd." The sign was his certification, the garage his atelier where he could keep his life and work simple as he restored dented surfaces to their original shapes. By seven each morning, he was gone from the house, the door shutting quietly behind him, a peanut butter sandwich in his pocket. At the garage following an evening snowfall, his were the first footsteps in the snow. After shoveling a driveway so that cars could enter, he unwrapped his sandwich and slowly ate it with intermittent sips of coffee. A peaceful time in the sanctuary, a full half hour before others arrived at eight and the sound of hammers and drills resounded through the smell of oil, turpentine and gasoline.

Whenever given a choice, my father preferred all aspects of his life to be unadorned. In the winter, when my mother spent a weekend in St. Agathe with her mother and older sister, my father was charged with preparing meals for himself, my brother, and me. But an elaborate table didn't figure into his conception of the good life. He served each course in succession on a single plate in order to reduce the number of dishes to be washed. The menu was simple— for breakfast oatmeal; for dinner, a steak on a grill. Nothing that required a fancy sauce or more than three steps. Anything more complicated he saved for the garage where his major ingredients were metal, a soldering iron, paint, and a sledge hammer.

His business card read "proprietor" and, although he must have taken pride in that title, he never really had the inclinations of a businessman, rather the instincts of an artist. And so he was relieved to resign bookkeeping to my mother's younger sister and later—when she gave up dressmaking—to my mother, whose prudence and judgment he increasingly relied on in any serious business decision. What he brought were not bookkeeping skills, but a deftness with tools. In the metallic world of smooth surfaces and dents, he had found his language. Over time, for instance, he contrived a series of bars attached to a rubber suction cup which was placed over a dent. Hammering a single post would jolt the others, pull on the suction cup and miraculously draw out the dent. But the thought of patenting and marketing this device never occurred to him. His mind never turned in those directions.

Now in a garage of his own, my father had found his milieu. And yet, what lurked beneath the surface was always a threat. Earlier, he had navigated through difficulties with utter confidence: moving through enemy lines as a child during World War I to rediscover his family, running with pilfered fruit from an orchard as soldiers fired at him, moving from village to city, finally leaving home as a teenager and transporting himself to a new world; but the Depression which brought him and a whole continent to their knees taught him what the soldiers shooting at him never did. The world was uncertain, could collapse under your feet, undo the magic of your hands. So he discovered when he returned to Montreal after visiting his brother in New York, and found the auto body shop he'd worked at empty, his boss seated on an orange crate. In the years that followed, he took whatever jobs he could find—once delivering coal, and, later, chickens before hiring on as an auto body repairman at Chevrolet Motors in 1933 and six years later at Latimer Motors.

He survived the Depression and by 1946 had even saved enough to buy some lakeside property seven miles north of St. Agathe, in Nantel. Its surrounding mountains breaking into fields at one end of the lake reminded him of Yurkovitz, opening up for him a feeling of permanence and belonging. As he sat in his row boat, fishing rod in hand, surrounded by water and greenery, his ample house set on a rise, he felt safely circumscribed.

But pastoral settings alone would never provide him with certainty and the deepest sense of belonging that he needed. Intuitively he reached for the family that he had left behind in Romania and who were now scattered. To his mother in Czernowitz, he sent a portion of his wages. To his brothers Meyer and Motl in the United States and Rudolph in Peru he sent brief letters, less from a desire to pass on news than a need to assert that the family was intact.

A Peruvian cousin once described my father and uncles as titans,

Brothers Uncle Motl, Father, Uncle Meyer, late 1940s.

more mythic than real, figures who scrambled onto the shores of another world and forged lives for themselves.

In a photo of my father, Motl, and Meyer, taken in the late 1940s on a park bench near my Uncle Meyer's apartment in the Bronx, I see something less than titanic. Scoured by their North American experience, they have been resculpted as mere humans.

My father sits in the middle. To his right, Motl, the oldest brother, who, after being fired for organizing a union as a teenager, emigrated from Czernowitz, living first in Philadelphia, before settling finally in New York. He has acceded to a request that he pose for this picture, but his attention is elsewhere. Sheltered within the formality of his clothing—suit and tie, the uniform of his profession as financial consultant—he now lives in two worlds, but feels no need to reveal much of either one. His brothers know little of what he passes on to financiers at Walston & Company; and to those who wait for his pronouncements on the stock market, he gives up nothing about his family or about what lies within the covers of books that line the shelves of his apartment. Pensive, the most speculative of the family, he has long ago abandoned activism, and, often alone, has carried on a dialogue with those tenants on his shelves who have written on history, philosophy, astronomy, and religion. Aware of imperfections around him and in himself, Uncle Motl has retained an ability to chuckle at the absurdities of the world, to take pleasure in assemblages of family even when limited, as in this photo, to only two brothers, and to delight in the inquisitiveness of children. Hyman and Sylvia, the children of his younger brother, Meyer, were vessels to be filled with affection and wisdom. He drew close to them not by entering their childhood, but by drawing them into his adult world: guiding their reading from nineteenth century novels to Heinrich Graetz's *History of the Jews*, explaining the panorama of early man at the Natural History Museum, and bringing them to concerts at Lewisohn Stadium, where Sylvia recalls how the opening bars of the chorale in Beethoven's Ninth Symphony sent her "up in glory."

On the other side of my father is my uncle Meyer. He has removed his jacket and folded it over the park bench. The sun is out and he would like to feel it on his arms, which were usually covered by heavy sleeves when, as a machinist at United Metal, he was one man among many on a conveyer line, deafened by sounds of grinding wheels and powdered by layers of dust rising slowly from the damp concrete floor. The tension he carried away from the plant was what adults, especially those outside the family, saw, but with children he was entirely at ease. It seemed as though he could step backwards into his past until he became a child among children, delighting in our play. He couldn't resist the games of the neighboring children in summer bungalows, adding some of his own, such as imaginary trials which he supervised with a smile tucked behind a mask of judicial severity.

Meyer's work as a machinist gnawed at his energy, but not his passion, which he brought to the study of history. For Motl, history happened at a distance so that his interpretations had the air of scholarly detachment. Meyer was closer to history's narratives, as close as it is possible to be without being an actual participant. And they transformed him. I remember the twistings of his mouth as he explained the intricacies of Scipio Africanus' strategy against the invasion of Hannibal and the grimness that his face acquired when he described the Romans sowing the Carthaginian fields with salt after the battle of Zama. In the photograph, with hands folded, he looks beyond the photographer, as if seeing no mere landscape, but a series of hardships and considering the resolution necessary to confront them.

Casually attired, one hand on his lap, the other at his side, my father maintains the beginnings of a smile that he brought to most occasions. Because his economic worries are fewer than they used to be, he is content to live in the present; and so the study of history that so absorbed Motl and Meyer engages him only occasionally, and then, primarily as a curiosity. The only time I would see him shaken was years later on a winter day when the weather made us hunker into additional layers of clothes, our parkas zipped tightly, with scarves around our faces, and ear flaps down. I knew something was wrong when he returned not in the evening as he usually did, closing the garage after the last customer finished his gossip, but a couple of hours early. Not merely that, he had no overcoat on, only the long tan smock and cap that he wore in the garage. That day the smock had an odd smell to it; I noticed that its edges were scorched. "I'm ruined" were the only words he was able to utter for several minutes as he sat down at the kitchen table and stared into the twilight. It had finally come home to him. In the midst of all that prosperity, disaster which he first knew as a child, had never really given up. It had grown, enlisted its own soldiers, built its own capital, waiting for the propitious moment, which finally arrived—a spark igniting a small pool of gasoline that spread into a blaze. Before the fire consumed everything, he managed to drive several vehicles out into a lot. But others were destroyed.

As it turned out however, the calamity was not as shattering as he had assumed. Rather than take their cars to other garages, his clients waited patiently until he was able to bring his hammer to the task. Years later, the legal action that he dreaded was taken by Simpson's department store, his major client, on the grounds of negligence.

Lawyers and their official sheets of paper always held a terror for him, as they did for other immigrants, who saw them as the invisible hands of a government raised against their aspirations. He was more comfortable with a frank discussion and a handshake. A lawyer couldn't be trusted to be on your side, and when he smiled, put his hand on your shoulder, nodded in agreement, you worried the most. My father had not forgotten that he was an alien presence with no passport, no official papers. Questioned by the Royal Canadian Mounted Police about his credentials, which were bought, he wouldn't be shaken. But they left unsatisfied, threatening to return. For him authorities in uniform were never the representatives of law and order, but enemies, not to be trusted. He'd keep his own council.

It is 1991, late August, and I am alone in the back seat of an Opel driven by my host, Eva, her mother beside her, and, in the rear view mirror the University of Warsaw where I have just given a poetry reading. Eva is half Jewish, which is known to no one but her mother and husband, and, in a stretch for kinship, to me. She has agreed to drive me to Gora Kalwaria where my mother spent her first twelve years. I am eager to see where my mother lived, but realize that the chances of identifying her last home in Poland are slight. My only hope is to find someone who lived there before the war, a surviving Jew, though the chance of a slip in Nazi thoroughness is unlikely. Along the main street we notice an old man warming himself against a spread of sunshine on a stucco wall. He is curious about the car that stops in front of him, and in response to Eva's questions offers the name of someone who might know my mother's family, the town butcher, Feliks Karpmann. Karpmann is one of the town's four surviving Jews, in his case having escaped from a concentration camp and been recaptured, but then freed when the Soviet army drove the Nazis out of Western Poland. He is now one of the few local residents who can describe the Jewish history of the town to Jewish visitors.

He walks briskly, pointing out buildings, commenting to Eva until his voice blurs into a soporific hum, but what she translates prods me into my mother's world. He identifies three houses where my mother might have lived. They look alike, dull yellow with windows that are dwarfed by the heaviness of the surrounding stucco. Nondescript, sullen, they reveal nothing of their past to the outside world, even to those who have made the pilgrimage from the distance of two generations. I am unable to conjure anything that might have happened within them, to envision the large room in which my mother, aunt, and grandmother slept beside the sewing machine that provided their meager income. My mother had mentioned a cellar where the family huddled when soldiers roamed the streets, but these houses, smug in their firmness and forbidding, still refuse to yield to the probing of my imagination. The synagogue, Karpman reminds us, is no longer a synagogue. At one time it ministered to the needs of its Jewish population of three thousand, among them my mother. Now something only slightly larger than a telephone booth might suffice. This is where my mother lay on the floor, terrified, when troops fired bullets through the windows. Prostrate on her stomach, she felt something wet against her finger tips. Turning her head, she saw an expanding rim of red and knew that her friend beside her, motionless, would not move again. Karpmann insists that this synagogue will open again as a Jewish museum; after all it was once a center for Hasidic Jews who danced in the surrounding streets. My mother remembered these men in long dark coats with broad brimmed hats, side burns and beards, who spoke loudly and gestured wildly when they filled the streets of Gora Kalwaria on Passover, Rosh Hashanah, and Yom Kippur. There is an edge of pride to Karpmann's voice as he tells Eva that he has taken on the function of keeper of the Jewish cemetery, a task that began for him immediately after the war when he excavated the headstones that the Nazis had used to pave roads and returned them to the cemetery.

Jews being marched from Gora Kalwaria to the Warsaw Ghetto.
Courtesy of Feliks Karpmann.

As we walk slowly along the main street, he gives me two photos as reminders of my visit here. The first is a picture of the Gora Kalwaria rabbi and other Hasids. The second is a photo of Jews being marched along the street on which I am standing, on their way to the Warsaw Ghetto, about twenty five miles away. How many met their end there or at Treblinka? Or were found in heaps when the camps were finally liberated? Even Eva, who is closer to this saga, is struck as I am at the nearness of it all, at how the past has come out of a photograph and grabbed us by the lapels. As she looks at this photo again, as if trying to locate something familiar from among the figures carrying enormous sacks, I turn to leave her a private moment and notice on a wall behind me a poster advertising an Arnold Shwarzenegger movie with the caption "Soon the hunt will begin." I am transfixed by the blank pitilessness on that face, its serenity of pure destruction. The street is quiet except for some hints of children at the fringes of our attention, and I nudge Eva, inviting her to share this moment when life moves from random chaos to something that seems painfully ordered, like a play or a nightmare. She nods.

The cemetery has become Karpmann's sanctuary. He maintains it as best he can, aware that none of the dead lie beneath their corresponding headstones. For him it is enough that they assert a presence in this pastoral setting with cows munching on tufts of grass and sparrows hopping from twig to twig, feathering the afternoon. Sitting in the back seat of the car, on my way back to the Europa Hotel in Warsaw, I begin to scrawl some lines shaped by my voyage to my mother's childhood.

At the Jewish Cemetery in Gora Kalwaria
  –for Feliks Karpmann who rebuilt the Jewish cemetery

There are no hills here, the war
flattened them, peeled
the earth like lemon rind releasing
mists that twist through earth

in Hebrew characters
on these stumps of stone;
in neighboring fields
sparrows fly
aimless as tourists.

My mother remembered part of it,
an earlier part: how she clung
to the synagogue floor like a crab
when armies passed through and bullets
splintered the walls; her friend
in blood loosened her grip.

By the cemetery, roadside flowers
rise to attention
by slopes of willow, invading
scrambles of weeds.

I am handed a photo I pluck
to life with my fingers: Jews marching
from one margin to the other, beyond
the photo to Warsaw's ghetto, carrying
flour sacks stuffed with blankets
past a house owned by Borenstein—my mother's

mother?—who lathered her kitchen with laughter
and sang eggs into cake batter.
They carried their sacks
beyond this MEBLE sign
where my uncle baked bread and gossip.
On a poster behind glass, Arnold
Schwarznegger bulges
as predator in black
letters "Soon the hunt will begin."

Here where the cemetery wall stood, they
were lined up, those who hid
in cellars, in tall grass, surfacing
like frogs on marsh lilies
to be plucked by birds with long beaks.
After a few bursts they became
Poland; the cows
in neighboring fields did not
stir.

And tanks passed over once,
twice, a finale. Headstones lay
like corpses in the camp yard
lathered over with paving tar.

This is what Feliks found,
the town butcher who separated
meat from meadow sounds
into cubes and strips,
who released the stones,
arranged them by height
or alphabet or age.

They blaze like shattered
diamonds on emerald
soft as cloth or meadow,

a gift for anyone
who leaves the road
and walks among stones
that have found their soil
but will not remain silent.

As far back as I remember, it was my mother's voice that broke
the silence in our flat. Perhaps in Gora Kalwaria her voice might
have been muted by the poverty of table scraps, the fear of shattering glass in a synagogue, and, later, in Montreal, the humiliation of
sitting in a classroom with English, her new language, spoken so
deftly by the other children, turning in her mouth to ugly bulbous
sounds. Later on she noted, with pride, some few moments of as-
sertion in her childhood—organizing plays as well as a home lend-
ing library—although these opportunities had been limited. But
the compulsion to arrange the space around her, whether moral or
aesthetic, grew as she grew into adulthood.

Having endured anti-Semitism in her native town, she had a
sense of when she could and could not act, of where the line was
drawn. But if provoked she would cross it. One late fall, a peddler was making his way with horse and wagon down Clark Street.
Was he sharpening knives, buying rags, selling rags? It could have
been any of those activities carried out by immigrants even into
World War II. A policeman, broad shouldered, tall, unable to pass
up the opportunity of demonstrating the superiority of a native
born Quebecer, and, to boot, a Quebecer in official uniform, took
out his book of tickets to cite the peddler for a traffic violation. The
peddler's stammering protest in a mixture of English and some
Slavic language had no effect; the policeman continued to write.
The scene took place in front of the window at 4112 Clark where
my mother was seated at her sewing machine. She dropped the

fabric in her hand and tripped quickly down the porch stairs. She was haranguing the policeman before she reached him. Scarcely five feet tall, she was no more than a dwarf against the frame of the policemen, but with her mouth spitting rage, she must have seemed like a pit bull, possibly rabid and not to be crossed. When the policeman had retreated to the end of the block, my mother returned to her sewing machine, with hardly a glance at the peddler. On that day, there may have been lunacy in the rest of the world, but on Clark Street between Rachel and Duluth, justice was in the driver's seat.

Like most immigrants sprung from poverty, my mother's disposition was first to establish a domain, then to extend it: first to rent a flat, make it habitable, provide for her children and send them to university; then to buy a home and furnish it according to her long held concepts of the beautiful. Whether as a renter or owner, she preferred large well-lit rooms. Darkness and confinement reminded her of huddling in her cellar in Gora Kalwaria or under the seat in the synagogue with bullets spearing through the walls. Her taste in furniture aimed at convention, with some attention to comfort, a preference for polished hard woods, cherry or mahogany, lamp bases and serving platters with pastoral scenes innocuous enough to give no offence to visitors. Once, when a lamp had an element of design that could be construed as a cross, my father was called in to obscure it with gold paint.

As she sat in her living room at 4112 Clark Street in 1946, twenty-three years after her ocean passage, it must have occurred to her how much her life had changed. She had just signed a purchase agreement for a house in the Laurentians on a lake. And she was beginning to ask about houses in other more affluent parts of the city. (Our neighbors had not yet disappeared into these more affluent suburbs, but there were stirrings.) For the first time, she went into supermarkets without having to husband her cash or compare prices. Yet, when coupons appeared in the newspapers, she continued to cut them out. She saw their appearance as an act of grace as well as an invitation to bury memories of scarcity as she filled up her pantry at bargain prices.

The routine around the household had also changed. Miss Bonnehomme, who had stayed over on Saturday evenings, was now around on weekdays as well, helping my mother with her sewing. After she revealed that she played the piano, my parents acquired an upright, and in the living room facing the street, Miss Bonnehomme undertook to transfer to us children her elegant fingering of the keys. My brother took to it immediately, and willingly practiced his scales and any other exercises that Miss Bonnehomme would contrive. My piano career ended abruptly. During the first lesson the street noises of the neighborhood children and the pock of tennis balls against the lumber yard wall informed me that activities were taking place for which I was more fit. As soon as Miss Bonnehomme turned her head I bolted towards an open window, and before she could cross the carpeted floor I had wedged myself through the opening and was running down the street. A gentle lady, Miss Bonnehomme restrained herself from screaming after me; nor did my mother direct me back to the piano stool. Sensing that there was too much anarchy in me to be governed by piano exercises, she saved her energy for more important battles.

Dressed in her smock, my mother concentrated on guiding fabric through the click-clack of her Singer, and, with Miss Bonnehomme as her assistant, prepared the dresses, suits, and gowns that her customers tried on. "Fittings" my mother called them. With an air of total concentration, she walked around her clients, scrutinizing them as an architect would a building, looking for imperfections, and when she detected one, a drooping hem or snug shoulder, she removed one of the pins from between her lips and stuck it into the appropriate place. Her day in the sewing room was done when my father returned from work, usually between six and seven in the evening, had a single shot of whiskey, and sat at the kitchen table. Dinner was an occasion for devouring food rather than conversation. Occasionally, she returned to her machine to finish a garment.

When her evening was free we took our accustomed places in the family car as soon as the dishes were put away and drove to the eastern extremity of the city, passing by Lafontaine Park so that we could see the fountain gushing in a multitude of colors. I came to realize that these drives had their origins in the strolls up and down the main street of a town that our ancestors customarily took. Driving was my mother's way of demonstrating that it was no longer necessary to stroll, that we could afford a car.

The chronic uncertainty that beset my father peeled from my mother in layers the longer she stayed in Montreal and the more her speech shed the accent that would identify her as a greenhorn. Gradually she approached virtually every subject from home design to sewing to vacations with confidence. No longer would the world cause her doubt or hesitation. Her circle of friends, both those she knew from the old country and those she met in Montreal multiplied, people with strange names like Louis the Skunk, named for the furrier's trade he practiced, and, weekly, she met with a group to play a game that fascinated me—mah-jongg. It seemed incongruous that these women, immigrants themselves or the daughters of immigrants, married and freshly out of the factories, should be arranging tiles with elegant Chinese characters. Their background conversation grew louder as each of the ten women chose to add her voice to the others. When the game ended and they shifted to tea and whatever sweets the hostess had provided, the volume rose to a crescendo. Anyone approaching the house would hear those voices from a block away. But it did not trouble them. They were no longer immigrants, sheltered within families. They were now confident enough to declare their belonging. Their children might blush with embarrassment at the mayhem of sound, but they had done with being subdued.

Our old neighborhood divided itself between those who organized their lives around religious orthodoxy, a distinct but obtrusive minority, and others who didn't. Since my parents had both experienced privation as children, the abstemious lives of the orthodox family upstairs had little attraction for them; they would not be constrained by a morality that they saw as unnecessarily austere. More-over, the rancid kitchen smells that sank to our first floor and the unkempt red beard of the family patriarch spreading like a stork's nest reminded my parents of the disease and poverty that they had known in Europe. The extent of their religious observance was no more than what would be expected by those within their circle. For example, my mother never combined meat and dairy products in the same meal, but did not keep separate dishes for each. She was taken by new fashions in cuisine, especially Chinese, popular in Montreal after World War II, never inquiring as to whether these conformed to orthodox Jewish dietary laws. She retained enough revulsion to the products of a pig so that she would never eat or fry a pork chop that could stare up accusingly from the frying pan. But when spare ribs submerged in garlic sauce accompanied other Chinese dishes, she stripped the bones until not a shred of meat was left. It never occurred to her that the source of her pleasure might previously have been sniffing around chewed ears of corn and a variety of other slops, chomping out a symphony of grunts.

As my father gained more customers the family savings grew. It was no longer necessary for my mother to coax her sewing ma-chine into its up and down chatter, but the habit of work, built over the years, made her uncomfortable with absolute leisure. By the time I left Baron Byng, she had taken over minor clerical duties at my father's shop, first answering the telephone and, before long, sending out invoices. The little luxuries that she never would have permitted herself, she now acquired: a mirror with ornamented borders and a platter with a pastoral scene copied from Watteau. She was no longer the woman who sprang from her sewing machine to confront a po-liceman on behalf of a peddler. Perhaps if such a situation had pre-sented itself that moral explosiveness might have returned. But she was now sheltered from the world of the peddler and found security and ease of mind in her daily phone calls to her sisters and mother, and in fellow volunteers working for Jewish organizations. No lon-ger in her sewing smock, but in a suit she'd sewn herself, she helped to organize raffles for Israel or the Baron de Rothschild's Institute. Prominently displayed on her living room wall was an autographed picture of herself receiving a certificate of appreciation from Justice Harry Batshaw on behalf of the Combined Jewish Appeal. Her concerns had shifted from her own survival to the survival of the family, and finally, to the larger community of her people—not other Canadians, but Jews wherever they came from.

I am holding two photos that I have recently removed from a family album. They were taken in Israel when my parents, then retired, took a long anticipated trip, probably with the same mixture of feelings that pilgrims in the Middle Ages carried to the Holy Land. In one my parents are leaving the Wailing Wall where Jews still wedge between blocks of stone scribbled messages—"kvitlech"—that plead for, among other favors, good health and successful marriages. With the wall at their backs, they are holding hands, something they rarely did. Neither of them had the conception of love that has made its way into popular song. Their expressions are enigmatic. They are not wailing although they had known the hardship of being Jews in alien lands. Perhaps the pilgrimage to the wall was a way of acknowledging the often sad history of their people, of saying that despite the good fortune that allows us to travel and touch this wall, we remain touched by it, both the wall and the history it represents. In the other photo, they are leaving Yad Vashem, Israel's memorial to the victims of the Nazis. My father is walking ahead, two or three steps at the most, but he and my mother are separated, lost in their own thoughts, linked to their own pain. Both look stricken. As though they had just learned of a catastrophe in the family or been jolted from a deep sleep and battered. Yet they had long been aware of the Holocaust. They'd had hints of it during the war, and after the war the truth emerged, first in a trickle, then in a burst, with a barrage of photos of emaciated arms and legs pushed by tractors into mass graves. Safe in Canada, they had spent their years in moving through French Catholic and English Protestant worlds, their Jewishness often no more than

Parents at the Wailing Wall (top) and Yad Vashem (below).

gestures—occasional holiday meals, a Jewish newspaper, charitable work. But Yad Vashem made them aware of a wall that had always existed between them and the abutting gentile world and raised that wall a little higher.

Although my mother exchanged pleasantries daily with non-Jews, mainly those in my father's garage, she did not seek them out, but in two cases, had relationships with gentiles that were not merely close, but familial. It is impossible to enumerate Miss Bonhomme's many functions in our household, among them piano teacher, baby sitter, and assistant seamstress, always around, often in her corner in my mother's sewing room, adding some pleasantry about the weather or my brother and me, making sure by the end of the conversation, that the intercession of God was properly invoked. She laughed, moved softly from room to room, spreading her glow in all seasons, and never failed to send birthday cards to my brother and me with silver sprinkles that reminded us of her as they gradually detached and fell to the floor. The other adopted gentile member of our family was Ulysse, an adolescent when my father took him on at the garage. Year by year Ulysse learned the techniques of shaping fractured metal, and eventually became my father's partner. He dealt with my parents as if they were his own, seeing to it that my father carried less of the work, but enough so that he never lost his view of himself as a craftsman. And they in turn saw him as a son. Whenever my mother brought lunch to the garage for my father, usually something that could be found in a Jewish cook book, she always brought the same for Ulysse.

As her life moved beyond calamity and unpredictability, she seemed less troubled, quicker to laugh; still, she occasionally brooded, as though something unforeseen might threaten all she had built. Most hazards she could foresee and ward off through thrift, insurance, and sound judgment. But managing my brother and me was a challenge, even to those three safeguards. She envisioned a prosperous future for both of us as members of a profession, married, with children, but she was not entirely sure about the route to that future. Although she had seen enough of education to know that academic success was one step on the way, the quirky paths of individual difference puzzled her. My brother and I were not like the children of my mother's circle, who would follow the customary paths into law, engineering, and medicine. My brother continued his piano lessons and developed a passion for music that extended to other activities, ultimately to composing and painting. Although he had a natural inclination to mathematics, he had no desire for a career built on numbers. My mother was not sure what he would do to earn a living, and her uncertainty troubled her. A vocational counselor suggested accounting as a career. My brother chose civil engineering, but has spent his life composing and listening to music, hiking the trails of several continents and observing flora and fauna miles from the old neighborhood.

I was more of a problem. Although I continued to enjoy reading, and mastered enough science and math to get through my final years of high school, I had a habit of falling into academic chasms. On one occasion my grade in physics was so low as to prompt a stern warning from the principal. This was enough to drive my mother into action. While she did not understand the chemistry of motivation, what she did understand—numerical and letter grades—she addressed with her usual vigor. She was not given to hesitation and conscripted my cousin to tutor me in physics. His disapproving expression, and he always approached with the same expression, kept me in terror. I still remember the material he taught and even now can convert centigrade to Fahrenheit. My brother had his share of tutoring as well, and as a result, we both went on to university.

Now, as old as my mother was when she died, I try to understand her brooding. She had, after all, found her "good life" whether in Montreal, the Laurentians or, later on, a condominium in Florida, all places where she could lounge and find abundance in her refrigerator and freezer. Perhaps she was no different from all of those others who had come before or followed her, scrambling to make a life for themselves, yet finding something that could not be overcome by fewer working hours, stuffed refrigerators or country homes. There was always something in the distance that gnawed at the abundance she had created, a remainder of uncertainty. Not so much for herself, but for others. How would the world deal with her children, their children? Would they be resourceful, prudent enough to herd their offspring from danger?

Shifts

THE TIME ITSELF was confusing. Earlier, the newspapers had presented the globe as a moral allegory with good guys (Canada, of course, and the USSR) and bad guys (Germany and Japan). But their positions were beginning to shift. No longer caricatures of evil, Germany and Japan had become trading partners, friends. And the Soviet Union, which we had readily accepted as an ally of Canada and the United States against Hitler, admiring its doggedness at both Leningrad and Stalingrad, was now the pilot ship of a menacing ideology, which, according to our principal, Mr. Patterson, was steaming across the Atlantic at full speed.

In this period before Krushchev disclosed the nightmare of Stalin's gulag to the world, we were battered by three distinct messages. For Montreal's major newspapers, the *Star, Herald* and *Gazette*, the workers' paradise proclaimed by local communists was nothing more than a string of concentration camps. The Soviets were not to be trusted. Hadn't they signed a pact with Hitler before the war? And according to our premier, Maurice Duplessis, communism was not merely a political party, but a satanic instrument intended to corrupt French Canadians. But despite such formidable opposition, the party retained a following in Canada. Our representative, Fred Rose, and the Communist leader, Tim Buck, insisted that the leading newspapers were simply instruments of the political bosses, people on the wrong side of every issue, who sent others to die for their interests. A third voice steered between the two. Suspicious of what was going on within the Soviet sphere of influence and mistrusting what it couldn't see, it still remained skeptical about the aims of the Western powers. These were the views of the radical newspapers, oracles that popped up from under the counter at Nathan's, where hot dogs had gone up to ten cents. Skeptical himself, Nathan perched outside the circle of political commitments and responded to any expression of patriotism, certainty, idealism, and enthusiasm with a benign smile that occasionally dipped to a sneer. Still, the articles in these newspapers aroused the curiosity of us students who had been harangued in history classes with the blessings of the empire and the glories of the factory system. In the meanwhile, my father followed the news in the daily paper without indulging in an overdose of analysis. Like many of his neighbors, he did bring a Russophilic sentiment to his judgment of political events, thus concluding that the United States generally affiliated itself with oppressive regimes. He was for the underdog.

Though our predominantly Jewish riding had elected Fred Rose, the Labor Progressive (communist) Party candidate, to Parliament, it was not politically homogeneous, and a discussion in Horn's or Gittleman's Barber Shop would raise a variety of political outlooks. Many in the neighborhood had attached themselves to the American dream, Canadian style, convinced that by saving their pennies, they could buy the homes they occupied, acquire the shops where they practiced their trades, and send their children to university. Anti-Semitism had dwindled to the point where most sectors of the economy were open to Jews. They had more material choices than their parents, and many of them, including my parents, had high aspirations for their children, who, they hoped, would become doctors, lawyers, and engineers. McGill was close at hand, and, though a quota was placed on Jews, one might get there by scoring higher on the high school leaving exams than other applicants.

From time to time I was made aware by my parents that Baron Byng was merely a pause, that I was on a mission, which was not to end with a mere high school diploma. Though I had not settled on what I wanted to do for the remainder of my life, there was a tacit understanding that I would go on to university. This understanding wobbled when my mother inspected my report card, curling her mouth at my dismal grades as though she could raise them to respectability by simply twitching her mouth into the right position. But no matter how much her mouth twitched, I excelled at nothing. My discovery in high school was that I had little inclination for any academic area. I found far more comfort in the Rachel Street poolroom and in daydreaming, but assigned readings at Baron Byng High did sometimes stir my imagination. In my first high school years, London's *Call of the Wild* summoned memories of the early days of Canadian sorties into the wilderness and made me yearn for more adventure. And Shakespeare's *As You Like It* as well as the King James version of the Bible, were introductions to a language I had not heard—voices deep, sonorous, clearly from a past to be cherished, an invitation to read further. Although several teachers, content with paraphrasing meaning, persisted in cutting the blossoms from the text, I discovered that by mere sustained interest, I could restore the bloom to those passages. The words were familiar, at least most of them were, but their arrangements were like thunderclaps and impressed upon me how craft could raise the grain from sheets of literature.

After two years at Baron Byng, it became clear that my grades as they stood would not get me admitted to a university, and so my parents, who rarely nagged about homework, determined that they had to intervene. Since my lowest grades were in math, they decided that they would hire Mr. Zweig to tutor me first in algebra, then geometry and, finally, trigonometry. Mr. Zweig soon found the means to clarify the mysteries and chanciness of algebraic problems. With swift strokes of a newly acquired ball point pen, I found myself translating verbal descriptions of cars traveling at different speeds and mixtures with different percentages of fat into algebraic equations. Geometry also shed its mysteries and turned from a torment to a pleasure. Theorems inched to coherence, so that the exercises based on them had a sense of inevitability almost painful in its delight, much like observing a lie trying to wiggle itself back into the comfort of darkness while truth raced after it like a cheetah. Even trigonometry, so intimidating when I first opened the text and saw unrecognizable words like "sine" and "secant," with only the slightest effort yielded to equations in which one drew a line to cancel out equals and which produced baldly simple results. I enjoyed especially the problems that featured a boat at sea and an unknown distance to a lighthouse. The pleasure was not so much in solving the problem as in its remoteness from the practical world. The classroom suddenly became less important than this tableau of an open sea, the waves conveniently flat so that a seaman could get a clear view of the lighthouse, the sky's soft blue, with the sun in full blaze, highlighting the lighthouse in the distance, the slight angle from the pitch of the bow to the top of the lighthouse, all of this beyond the concern of the lighthousekeeper who might at the time have been occupying himself with a chess puzzle, an O'Brien novel about some sea battle, or an afternoon nap. It was like entering a setting where the familiar and unfamiliar come together, where enough is familiar so that one is not overwhelmed by the sensation of seeing something for the first time, but not overly familiar so that one sees nothing and drifts into unrelated fantasies.

Nantel

LONG AND COLD, Montreal's winters must have discouraged the early settlers. In a just world temperate weather would follow as compensation, but Montreal's springs are brief and its summers hot, humid, and debilitating. As a result, as soon as the public schools close down in mid-June, thousands of families evacuate the city for the Laurentians, a gentle mountain range that gradually rises from the St. Lawrence plateau thirty-five miles north of the city. Like their fellow immigrants, my parents, seeking refuge from the heat, and, especially in the 1940s and 1950s, from the threat of polio, joined the long line of cars. In 1946, unenthusiastic about the prospect of another summer in a rental shack at Préfontaine or Val Morin, they set out to look at some available property on a lake north of St. Agathe.

After a mile of navigating the deep ruts of a single lane dirt road overhung with foliage, my father concluded that the lake was inaccessible and turned back. We had not made it to the Promised Land, but, we soon learned, we had come within a quarter mile of it. And so, the following week we pushed further up the dirt road that branched from the Laurentian highway to discover a lake and on it a green house with a sloping roof and cedar shingles that I was to return to for the next forty years. With porches at either end it was more imposing than anything we had rented, and, shielded from the road by birches, maples, oaks, and pines, it was inviting, cool, and would shelter us, even on a hot afternoon.

The dirt road continued past three more houses perched above the shoreline before circling the end of the lake, where it separated the property of a beer bottler from that of a pianist, whose log cabin peeked through a thicket of fir trees. Two hundred feet further, the road dwindled to a path and finally an impasse of undergrowth. From this point one could see our house directly across the lake set on a slight rise. Not a hundred yards from our lake was an artificial

"With porches at either end it was more imposing than anything we had rented."

one, the handiwork of the beer bottler, Brisette, whose office was in St. Agathe. I saw him only once—imposing, with a full stomach and a huge bald head, our Mr. Kurtz. Next to his property, which lay between the two lakes, the surrounding mountains dipped into a valley and the land opened. My brother and I explored it with the pianist, whose childlike restiveness drove him to investigate with the zeal of a cartographer mapping newly discovered terrain. Half running after his long strides, we passed fields of blueberries—I had never seen so many—with a profusion of cornflowers and golden-rod, a chirping choir of birds, and a cow's skull, but no human presence. The land must have been farmed in the not too distant past; it was still not entirely overgrown though the tall grass and saplings had begun to raise barriers against human intrusion.

Under the red shingled roof of our house I felt safely on the inside of things; the surrounding mountains, among the highest in the Laurentians, and the rough road would preserve the house as we found it. For years we lived without running water or electricity, relying on the pump in the sink, the black iron wood stove, the one-seater outhouse, and the Alladin lamp fueled by coal oil, which radiated rings of light. During storms, the sound of thunder multiplied over those houses within the mountains, a protective clamoring, one more sinister face that would keep outsiders at bay. And so we could count on days that ran into one another with no interruption other than my father driving up from the highway on Friday evening to begin his weekend escape from the smoldering heat of the garage. He celebrated his arrival by plunging into the bracing water of the lake like a bear, sounding out gibberish to insulate himself from the cold as the raised droplets of water hung in the air like exclamation marks.

The years in Nantel were different from our earlier stays at Lesage, where our days following farmer Leblanc's chickens, cows, horses and pigs were like farm vacations in childrens' books; nor were they like our stays in Prefontaine and Val Morin, where we shared our neighborhood with playmates so numerous that they seemed like one mass of screaming childhood. At Nantel we saw no children and few animals, except for the occasional bear and the skunk that had installed himself in the outhouse. There must have been others, but they kept the cover of the denser woods. Surrounded by mountains and forest, I realized that I was in a country with no neighborhood; my brother and I had no companions, except for books, the woods, the boat, the lake, the open field at the end of the lake. The few houses were with an exception or two separated from each other by trees and brush, and the sounds we heard were more likely to come from animals than neighbors. It was as though the mountains had held a conclave and agreed to keep the locale as pristine as it had been for generations, resisting anything that smacked of an urban world or that seemed quirky.

And yet Nantel's few residents were, if not quirky, unusual. The owner of the farm at the base of the mountain was the guardian spirit of the dirt road to the lake. Unshaven, with specks of grey in his waves of brown hair, spitting syllables around his one upper tooth, he greeted us whenever our car was within reach of his voice. Chickens clucked around his shoes, and we coveted the eggs they laid, hardly ever passing the barn without buying a dozen. He was one of Quebec's farmers, who, in addition to the usual farm chores, patched together a living from several diverse activities— selling wood, building cottages, repairing small wooden bridges, and maintaining the dirt road. His children seemed to be as numerous as his chickens, and he paid as little attention to the appearance of one as to the other. His English was limited; my parents had no French. My mother got around this problem by adding a French accent to her English speech, assuming that the adjustment would clarify what she said. It may have because Mr. Patry usually turned up to take care of requests: painting the exterior of the house, moving the outhouse, repairing the wooden shed. He had enormous strength and on one occasion he was called on to demonstrate it. Rains had reduced the dirt road to a flow of mud, and my father on his way back to Montreal was unable to free the wheels of his car, which had become deeply mired. Without stopping to take a deep breath, Mr. Patry simply raised the rear of the car and nudged it forward until the tires gripped the grassy edge. For me he was French Canada's Paul Bunyan. Years later, I came across a photo of Mr. Patry taken at his oldest son's wedding. Patry is wearing a suit, possibly for the first time. Beside him is his wife in her Sunday coat, stout, toothless, and severe, with an assemblage of friends and family that could have been selected at random from a bus or airline terminal. For a brief period, he had left his farm and joined the world.

In Nantel the house next to ours was uninhabited for many years, although on a few occasions I did see the owner, Mr. Mora, an elderly Spaniard with a stoop and a sad smile, either entering or leaving. As he stared at the lake, the leaping trout, the reflection of birches and oaks on the lake's surface, perhaps his mind drifted to other places where the voices were familiar and townsmen nodded when they met him. His house was as large as our own, cream colored with faded green trim and unusual Moorish windows. What hint was he sending out to the uninterested world? Through the glass of those windows did he envision the sad eyes of the last émigrés fleeing from

The wedding of Mr. Patry's oldest son. Parents at right, rows 5, 6.

Granada in 1492, destined to wander from the splendor they had created?

Our most unusual neighbor was the pianist who lived on the other side of the lake. He had been there for a few years before my parents appeared as fellow residents. It was unusual for anyone to spend winters around the lake, the temperatures often falling to twenty-five below. Only the bottler, Mr. Brisette, had a house that was built to withstand the cold. But the pianist had stuffed the cracks of his log cabin with hay, grasses, cloth, anything to keep out the paralyzing winds. In addition to the golden tones of the logs what was most noticeable in that one room cabin was his piano, large and imposing, a piano that one could envision on a concert stage. Since he'd built the cabin before the road had been extended to his property line, he'd had to move the piano across the lake on a barge. It seemed odd that a barge would make its appearance on this lake that usually saw only a canoe or two or, rarely, something with a puttering motor. Was there something shamefaced about this barge in the shadow of the trees overhead making this crossing, its water line higher than usual with the weight of the piano? It was, after all, leaving behind something that gave a distinction of pure eccentricity to the lake. Other hamlets had their assortments of curios—alcoholics, a former felon, a priest who collected butterflies—but a pianist whose notes sent Chopin to all parts of a barely inhabited lake was as memorable as a cattle skull on an open field.

My brother and I cherished our moments with the pianist since there were no other adolescents to share our days with. Although he never played for us, except for an occasional flourish on the keys to show his dexterity, he took us on long walks through the thicket of paths that led from the lake. He knew all of the places where clusters of berries waited to be picked. The pots of berries we brought home were quickly transformed into pies, pierogies, and any other form in which dough wrapped itself around clumps of blueberries, raspberries or blackberries. As we walked, warding off low hanging branches or thorny bushes, he noted the characteristics of the mosses at our feet and the sparrows and waxwings that flew overhead. He told us that he'd once owned a BB gun and raised it impulsively to shoot at a sparrow, assuming that he would never hit it since his gun did not shoot accurately. When he discovered the bird on its side, lifeless, he resolved never to raise a gun again. I wondered how often he'd told that tale, carried that albatross with him.

It must have been the lack of adult company that prompted the pianist to seek us out; this same lack of neighbors, of days without small talk, with no one to talk to but us, creatures of another generation, made him a welcome visitor for my mother. He'd often come around for tea and my mother's pastries, and we heard the piano keys less in those days. Finally, the keys stopped altogether. More and more people found their way up the dirt road, built houses, and added to the noise that carried across the lake. It was too much for his ears, which were accustomed to silence, broken only by bird calls and the sounds leaping from his key board. He stopped by briefly to tell us that he was leaving, and a few days later, when we walked around the lake and peeked through the window of his cabin, we noticed that the piano was gone. We didn't know how he'd moved it. We hadn't seen a barge. Later on we heard that he had moved thirty miles north to Devil's River. He'd bought half the frontage of a lake, and then, fearing that the farmer who owned the other half might sell to speculators, bought his half as well. The notes of the piano then fell on no ears but his own. One day, he had an attack of appendicitis. In pain, he drove his car to the base of the mountain at Nantel, dragged himself into the general store, where Mr. Tassé, newly retired from the Royal Canadian Mounted Police at age thirty-nine, drove him to the hospital at St. Jerome. He survives in memory as someone who brought music to our lake, suspended it from twigs, and returned with a rebellious appendix.

Like many of my classmates, I worked in Montreal during my last two summers of high school and therefore spent less time in Nantel. For my parents the lake remained the paradise that they had sought; for me, independence in Montreal during the week with my mother in Nantel and my father at the garage had the excitement of novelty. In addition to working part time at menial jobs, such as washing windows and moving office furniture, I found time to scatter balls around a tennis court or take in an afternoon movie, squinting as I exited into the brightness of the sun. I was no longer as firmly attached to Nantel as I had been during my first summer. Like many fathers who arrived on Friday, I became another weekend visitor, a guest, who had hitchhiked from the outskirts of the city. My new status as guest was reinforced when my father lit the stove on cold mornings and had oatmeal and hot coffee on the table before I stirred. It all seemed so precious, as I awakened to the sun slanting across the bed in the small room at one end of the porch, all screens and glass panes, with no obligation that kept me from breathing the morning air and staring at the glass surface of the lake. Even the trout were still asleep. Walking from the porch through the living room, a room no one used, and into the kitchen, was an arrival into sociability.

These are my best memories of a place that I had attached to longer than any other. It has taken its place behind me with an assortment of other memories, but it awakens when I look at a photo taken a year or so after my parents acquired the house by the lake. All four of us are standing on the landing, facing the house, the lake to our backs; behind us is the pianist's log cabin, and beyond his neck of woods, Brisette's private lake. The picture was taken when the surroundings of the lake were my playground, my labor-atory and field of inquiry. Perhaps to ward off the unforeseen I am wearing a rabbit's foot. Did I want this idyll to last forever? Forty years later, my mother dead, my father's memory gone with her, my brother, made

The family in Nantel, Quebec, 1947.

his way up the dirt road in the midst of winter on cross-country skis, gliding the last hundred yards to a familiar setting. Except that it no longer was familiar. The lake was more visible, his view of it unobstructed. The two houses, Mora's and my parents' were no longer standing. The truth, buried beneath a smooth covering of snow, was that they had burnt to the ground. It was not much later that the property was sold. It was all over, we realized; it had been all over for a long time. Over the years, the changes that had driven the pianist to seek other solitudes had continued. On my last visit, what had been Patry's farm was now a golf course. I tried to reckon it all up in a poem, all I could salvage from the years there.

At Lac Nantel

> The lake's level has dropped
> in a shift of wind; boulders poke
> their bullfrog eyes through shallows
> to branches lowering for reflection.
> This birch must have leaned
> all through June, its bark curling
> like the manes of horses
> which warmer months fingered,
>
> mouthing through, leeching
> the middle to softness until it lowers
> like a head in hay,
> pushed over at first gust.
>
> It takes such a lowering to raise
> the memory of the neighbor's
> weather vane—all that remains,
> except scorched timber and a cement block
>
> or the piano the lake's eccentric barged
> to his cabin, departed last fall
> with the pianist.
> Not even a note left behind,

his stretch of frontage bought
for golfers and a building fleet
of paddleboats churning in circles
through flotillas of algae

where half-sunken branches stiffen upwards
like inquiry or death or children
when a strange bell has rung
not knowing where to turn.

Exits

I am moving crab-like through the streets of my childhood. Stars dim over parked cars and emptied streets. The neighbors have departed. Blinds are drawn; houses, tired, have shut their eyes. No thwacking of skipping rope against sidewalk, no children's songs. Once familiar and freckled with the spots of wet sponge balls, the lumber yard wall is now as aloof as the side of a museum. Mount Royal Elementary School has become a mass of condos though it could be mistaken for a giant accommodation for purple martins, but there are neither martins nor twittering pupils. And the adjoining yard where the photos of my seventh grade graduating class were taken has also gone silent. So have the corridors and classrooms of Baron Byng High. Language itself seems to have flattened with nothing to tease it back to life except the facades of old dwellings that speak to us in a code of stairway swirls and false mansards.

The XM radio in my parked car returns me to the world of Jack Benny and The Shadow with characters brought to life momentarily only to remind me that they too have vanished along with the signs of familiar shops, the voices of family, and the political arguments at Nathan's. Even our Laurentian escapes, those endless fields and dark soils, have turned into strip malls and souvenir shops.

Winters have done their work to the concrete slabs of sidewalks, hardly any without cracks, like large wooden puzzle pieces that even clumsy infants can fit together to create a picture of autumn foliage or a fluffy terrier. But these pieces do not fit exactly. Thin spaces between them whisper that they will never again cohere; nor will my old neighborhood with its landmarks of my elementary and high schools. Yet those landmarks, with dates chiseled into their facades—1905 for Mount Royal, 1922 for Baron Byng—once assured us that nothing would ever change, that the great tent of neighborhood would shelter us forever, its borders enclosing a community where we belonged, the comfort it provided sealed in.

But family and neighbors slip away and with them permanence and certainty.

At first hardly noticed, a small apartment goes up on a vacant lot, another demolished to create an empty lot, until the street is flooded with change; and, finally, we realize that there is nothing that we can take from these precious grounds except memories, and we take them, unreservedly.

During my last year at Baron Byng, the beginnings of change had touched most of my classmates who were busily preparing themselves for college entry exams; I remained untouched, and my last year there was little more than a holding action. Although I had no assurance from any source, I assumed that some fortunate conjunction of circumstances would get me admitted to a college. Outside of frantic last minute cramming for high school leaving examinations, I went through those final months light-footed, playing tennis with a schoolmate, shooting pool with anybody, and having conversations with a few friends, activities far more pleasurable than intermediate algebra which I finally wrote off as a conspiracy against my sanity. In the meanwhile, I found myself more and more drawn to literature and history, fascinated rather than overwhelmed by the thickness of our eleventh grade text that covered history from the classical to the modern period, spreading along the way one anecdotal enticement after another.

As the news of my father's magical hands spread within the city limits, and more and more dented vehicles found their way to his garage door, my parents settled into a prosperity they had never known. When they had saved enough for a down payment, they surveyed several houses, accompanied by a distant cousin, who presented himself as a real estate maven and took pride in a life that had avoided work and allowed him to cultivate a supercilious glance, an oracular expression, and a taste for fedoras which he wore on his real estate calls even in the blasting heat of summer. He expressed his seriousness by first rubbing its brim, then his hawkish nose, after which he would either nod his approval or shake his head slowly, waiting until we were in the car once again before he explained his reaction.

The emigration of Jews from the old neighborhood had begun, first family by family, later like a flash flood, to suburbs that had larger plots of grass and houses detached from one another by at least twenty-five feet. It didn't matter that these burbs had been hatched in an architectural nightmare, with houses one much like the other, except for a dab of paint here, a tin Doric column there. My parents were a part of this movement. Notre Dame de Grace, their new suburb in the west of Montreal, had some old gracious houses with wainscoting and other features of an older vintage. But since my parents resisted anything old, which they saw as a

Brothers Irv and George in N.D.G.

161

remnant of European decrepitude, they chose one of the newer duplexes on Draper Avenue that had been built only a few years earlier. The newer brick, bright and garish, came in the currency of their expectations, along with a back yard of evenly mowed grass.

Awakened by memories of the orchards they had seen and the fruit they had coveted as children, they planted anything that had a chance of growing, taking great pride in their tomatoes as well as their apple trees. My father even ventured a peach tree, though the squirrels reaped that harvest for themselves; and when my father asked Mr. Caporicci, his occasional gardener, for advice, Mr. Caporicci, stooped from his long trek with his Italian unit from the Russian front, suggested that if he left apples on the ground the squirrels might accept them as tribute and ignore the peaches. They never did. And we finally resigned ourselves at 4555 Draper Avenue, our newly acquired home, to sharing our produce with them.

Eventually, my father's work lightened as he increased his staff, and at my mother's initiative, my parents bought a condominium in Deerfield Beach in Florida, an area that was as removed from their old Clark Street neighborhood as a cockatoo is from an orangutan. In her own distinctive way, my mother brought the two neighborhoods together by prompting a number of her friends to purchase units at the same time, thereby bringing their Montreal chatter during the winter months to a Florida setting of palm and orange trees. Their diversions remained as they had been in Montreal—the click of mahjongg tiles for my mother, cards for my father, though only occasionally. He was inclined to putter around, but since the condominium was maintained by an organization, there was less need to putter.

Meanwhile my brother had begun an engineering program at McGill, spending his first year at McGill's satellite, Dawson College, in St. Jean, Quebec. It was his first excursion away from the neighborhood and the family. It was not to be his last. Although engineering and computer work confined him to the insides of buildings, he fixed his course on moving to the outdoors away from buildings and technology. He was most comfortable when he was alone, walking paths where there were few human voices: the Appalachia Trail which he walked twice, the Pacific Coast Trail, the length of the British Isles, the stretch from the Hook of Holland through the Alps, around the Himalayas in Nepal. In all of those places, he found a congenial world in the flora he walked by and studied, learned its blossoms the way he'd learned musical chords, took note of the speech of birds until he was able to eavesdrop on their conversations. Whenever I taught the Anglo Saxon poem, "The Wanderer," in which the wanderer is conveyed by the Anglo-Saxon word "eardstepa," ("earthstepper"), I was reminded of my brother who had chosen to walk his own paths, to sketch and photograph them, and to speak about them to those eager to listen to someone who lived in two worlds.

My inattention to my classes in my senior year left me time to read Ibsen and Shaw and to approach girls, who fascinated and mystified me, and who were different enough to make me feel uneasy. One exception was Ruth, who had asked me to tutor her in algebra. Since anything involving numbers highlighted the depth of my incompetence, I was flattered, and, allowing my vanity to win the day over good judgment, I leapt to the task. I must have been successful because Ruth's score in our high school leaving algebra exam was twenty-five points higher than mine, the kind of gap that separates competence from idiocy. It may have been that from the start she was humoring me, entertaining herself by listening to my bumbling explanations. When we were not teasing algebraic problems into numerical expression, we walked, sat over coffee or soda, or simply enjoyed silence. I believe I spoke more often, somewhat uncomfortable when the background of silence became too dominant. Against that background, her words, spoken always softly, as if offered deferentially, were authoritative, and I accepted them that way. She never provoked the sexual excitement of Lili St. Cyr or the other strippers at the Gayety or even Miss Kastner, but there was a warmth and a sympathy to her as she walked, turning only occasionally with the hint of a smile. This mathematical courtship hinted that it was possible for a girl to be a friend in much the same way as were any of the boys in the Buzz Beurling Memorial Club.

Like many other daughters of the neighborhood, Ruth married shortly after leaving high school. I heard that her life, like so many, shifted between boredom and sorrow. Only in recent years have I seen her—perhaps two or three times—enough to remind me of how the years can alter a high school photo, but cannot remove its essential—in this case, a wistfulness and wisdom that drew insightful conclusions about the world even before she had lived through its experiences.

The photo of Shelley standing beside me at the high school prom highlights Shelley's painstaking craft at assembling herself, the hair stylist's final touch, a curl over the forehead, the top of her gown resting half way up her breast as if to suggest not so much that the satin was fatigued after a long climb, but that this was the point of titillation for Shelley, who had learned the steps that led to marriage. Hershy Caplan, who could always be counted on to bring his photographic skills to ceremonial occasions has arranged the couple—which includes me—so that boy and girl seem permanently paired and destined to take the next step and the next until their steps turn into a silent walk behind a baby carriage. Silence would have been the best outcome of our brief relationship because I can remember no utterance of Shelley's that was not entirely predictable in its substance, in its choice of words, and in their arrangement. She spoke softly, with a quiet laugh, as if she knew the few critical things about adolescent boys. Looking at Shelley in her prom gown, I imagine her standing there with neither gown nor underwear, without embarrassment or flamboyance. She had reached into my imagination and wrapped her fingers around the kindling that I had ignited for the Gayety Theater ladies. I could see the shedding of her gown, the disappearance of words, the fading of colons and semi-colons as she drew me into her universe, babbling out the imbecilities that would ultimately make me yearn for forty years of wandering in the desert. The image of a couple walking wordlessly behind a carriage must have had a chilling effect on me, because when the university became the center of my life, Shelley slipped away as though she had been covered by a season of snowfalls. Although she lived next door, our schedules prevented accidental meetings. I suspect she was as grateful for this as I was.

When I look at the records my parents left, their photos and post cards, it only rarely occurs to me that they might have struggled in their search for a mate. Did my mother feel more ambiguity than emperor penguins do when they shuffle around hordes of their own kind, listening for the honk that will send them into ecstasy? In old photos I always see them as providentially destined for each other, cast to play out the role of mate, and, my self-indulgent fantasy adds, the role of caring parent. And yet everything else in my overall impression of the neighborhood comes to me not as predestined but as haphazard as the movement of fireflies, lighting up here first over a railing, then there under a branch—love, girls, sensuality, friendship— never coming together in any coherent way. Even in something as fundamental as desire, convergence seems the result of something casual, like those penguins—the right honk at the right moment.

My final academic record at Baron Byng represented efforts that were casual, haphazard, like the career of a firefly, with a glint of insight here, a flash of intimation there. Its list of dismal numerical grades would not have led anyone with reasonable judgment to predict success, and while several of my classmates enrolled at McGill University, I found myself at Sir George Williams College, which I regarded as a kind of purgatory for the unprepared, one which I hoped would be temporary. The college, now a world-class institution, was then housed in the YMCA building that fronted both Drummond and Stanley streets. Who Sir George Williams was I never discovered, and before I roused the curiosity to do so I had transferred to McGill University for my second year. My only distinction in the years that I spent there was to have an academic career without distinction. The bits of discipline that I acquired at

Baron Byng vanished, but I was not uninterested. I had begun to discover a world that would replace the old neighborhood. It was populated by writers taught by Louis Dudek, who would later introduce me to poetry. My days were consumed by Goethe, Voltaire, Dostoyevski, Nietzsche, Joyce, and the lengthy list of other writers that Dudek required until we read ourselves close to blindness.

In the pauses between books, my memory would turn to the old neighborhood, sprinting around the corner to Katz's button shop or stopping by Labow's pharmacy, surveying the carved wooden shelves while Mr. Labow persuaded my father to buy some energy-building syrup. By now my relatives had scattered. My aunt Faige, from whose balcony we watched the floats of the Christmas parade, had moved to Snowdon, a suburb in which her thinning memory found no connections. My mother's youngest sister, Esther, the first one to break away, had joined her husband in California, and wrote endlessly about orange, tangerine and lemon trees. Only my grandmother remained in the old neighborhood. She seemed so much a part of it that we could not imagine her moving away without leaving behind a crater to mark the spot where she had lived. Most of the other old families on Clark Street had also moved away, and with one or two exceptions, I never saw them again. Nor, surrounded by the mound of books that I was devouring, did I miss them.

Years later, I do regret having missed voices that were well within my range of hearing. In confining my attention to literature written in English, I passed over the work of Jewish poets writing in my own neighborhood—J. J. Segal, Sholem Shtern, and Ida Maze. As a student poet at McGill, I became familiar with the poems of A.M. Klein, Irving Layton, and Miriam Waddington, all Jews from Montreal who wrote in English, which made their work accessible. But I am saddened at having missed the work of those Jews writing in Yiddish who spoke out of their loneliness to an audience of so few. The appearance of their poetry in a language that was neither English nor French constituted a wall, thick as that of a medieval fortress, which separated them from a larger audience. Even now, as their work appears in translation by devotees such as Pierre Anctil, I remain touched by their aloneness, by their separation from those who might have read, listened, and admired.

True separations come from something fundamental—a smell, a sound, a sight. In my mother's kitchen, the mixing of meat and dairy products was taboo though to me it had no moral implications; it was simply incongruous with the aesthetics my tongue had developed. But the exclusion of pork carried the gravity of a divine pronouncement. We could not imagine that those creatures who snuffed their way towards slops at Leblanc's farm, who made those piteous sounds under a knife blade, were going to make their way onto our plates. But early on I found myself drawn to a sandwich that consisted of the usual breads with a single leaf of lettuce, three slices of tomato, a slice of ham, and a scraping of mayonnaise. Prosaic as this combination might have been for Jews who had crossed the dietary frontier earlier, it was a treat for me, an approach to, though not a swallowing of, the forbidden fruit. Yet, once a wall begins to crumble, I found when chiseling away at the Berlin wall for souvenirs in 1992, chips come off more readily, sometimes in miniscule pieces but often in larger and larger chunks, and before long, I found the scent of bacon that wafted through the halls of the McGill student union as inviting as any of the breezes that wafted through my literary texts. It was inevitable that the next sensation would be the crunch of bacon, fried to a crisp, between my molars. But the last step was the steepest. A slab of pork, call it either cutlet or chop, confronted the issue most clearly. Where it was easy to dissociate bacon or ham from a pig (how could such delectables, after all, be connected to such foulness?), those off-white slabs proclaimed their barnyard beginnings without a hint of ambiguity. And yet the odors when I opened the heavy door of the student union in September became by early December inviting aromas that insinuated themselves into my nostrils ahead of anything else that rose from the stainless steel beds of the steam table. It was impossible to walk by and not notice those cutlets, lightly breaded and arranged in formation like the phalanxes of Caesar's army. In the chuckles of my imagination they appealed to both my gustatory lusts and my passion for history, especially those eras of conquest and adventure—Caesar's excursions into Gaul, the grand armée of Napoleon at Austerlitz, Wagram, Marengo—wonderful names all-attaching to those individual tanned warriors wedged together on that steam table, and, to boot, in military formation. It could not have been long into the new year before I chose the cutlet over the leg of chicken. I fumbled with my change, not bothering to count what the cashier had placed in my palm. Was it more than thirty pieces of silver? It didn't matter. With the first bite, I had crossed a line. Esau, we are instructed, sold his birthright for a mess of pottage, basic food, crushed cooked lentils with onions and garlic; in the dead of winter I sold mine for a breaded pork cutlet. I have yet to sort out the outcome of this exchange.

Postscript

MOVING BRISKLY through the Louvre to visit once more with Vermeer's astronomer and lacemaker, I find myself looking at a number of Dutch rural scenes. I am struck by the cows, by the understanding that their painters, whose names I cannot recall, have of them. They seem to be looking at something outside the frame, possibly something that once belonged to them, unimportant for us, but important for them, It teases me to the point where I survey what I have left behind, an enterprise as consuming as looking forward. Perhaps when we get too anxious about looking forward, too tired from making the effort, we look back. But looking back is also tiring. And finding meanings in heaps of old records, photos, the details in incomplete diaries is heavy labor. Sometimes we are rescued by the epiphany sprung from a significant event, a persistent memory, or something as casual as a film.

A film *March of the Penguins*, produced in France, played in recent years at American movie theaters that rarely show such documentaries. After all, documentaries normally have neither special effects nor the level of violence that appeal to large audiences. But something in that saga of emperor penguins plodding across seventy miles of ice and snow to mate, with a multitude of hardships to follow, appeals to those who continue to watch and listen to the strange noises of these creatures for almost two hours.

The penguins alert us to the spectacle we are about to witness when they first break through growing fissures in the ice. They wait for one another till all have surfaced: the malingerers skimming the shore line for a last fish, the playful ones nosing through the dark waters ahead, the aimless sprinters circling glints of light around the circle glowing from above. And after the last straggler has made it to the icy surface, they begin the trek to the traditional mating place, seventy miles away. Of course there is a rational explanation for it. The ice is thicker there and will not crack open to swallow the hatched eggs that are to come. A tradition. And because there are reasons behind such traditions, we attend to them; we accept even those that at first glance seem outrageous or foolish, fasting on holidays when we no longer believe, walking in a procession whose cause we have long abandoned. Forsaking all traditions seems risky, too much like floating aimlessly down the Niagara River with a sense that the Falls will soon be upon us. And so we plod ahead, as they do, huddling together more closely when a blustery wind becomes a blizzard and the falling temperature turns breath to ice sculpture. In lighter moments the penguins break their daily routine of plodding with belly slides along the ice. Then they rise and plod some more. It doesn't end until they have reached the place where their elders mated. Like them they also mate, then huddle together until the emergence of an egg, presiding over it until it hatches.

Looking back to that old neighborhood preserved in my photo albums, I continue to seek out adventures, anything of the high mimetic that I can scrape from my parents' experience. What I find is that these experiences are never three dimensional, more like chips of paint that remind me of but never replicate the day to day world of my childhood and adolescence. What I discover is that I laugh more often than I used to as I look at these 3"x5" presentations of my past, not with judgment, but with acceptance. Under even the most flattering lights our aspirations turn to pratfalls, our lopes to waddles, our needle-pointed dives to bellyflops, swelling with energy for a world we seek to change but, usually, only repeat.

Véhicule Press